SCALING START-UPS

THE CHALLENGES,
PITFALLS & STRATEGIES.

I0395935

RAJ RAMAN

INDIA • SINGAPORE • MALAYSIA

Notion Press

No. 8, 3rd Cross Street
CIT Colony, Mylapore
Chennai, Tamil Nadu – 600004

First Published by Notion Press 2021
Copyright © Raj Raman 2021
All Rights Reserved.

ISBN 978-1-63781-415-4

This book has been published with all efforts taken to make the material error-free after the consent of the author. However, the author and the publisher do not assume and hereby disclaim any liability to any party for any loss, damage, or disruption caused by errors or omissions, whether such errors or omissions result from negligence, accident, or any other cause.

While every effort has been made to avoid any mistake or omission, this publication is being sold on the condition and understanding that neither the author nor the publishers or printers would be liable in any manner to any person by reason of any mistake or omission in this publication or for any action taken or omitted to be taken or advice rendered or accepted on the basis of this work. For any defect in printing or binding the publishers will be liable only to replace the defective copy by another copy of this work then available.

This is a work based on the experiences, views and opinions of the author. Names, Organizations, places and incidents are either the product of the author's imagination or are used fictitiously, and any resemblance to any actual person, living or dead, organization, event or locale is entirely co-incidental.

CONTENTS

Dedication & Acknowledgements *7*

Message from The Sponsor *9*

About SP-TBI. *11*

Prologue *13*

Chapter 1 – The Start-up DNA 17

> A germ of an idea, distilled with coffee and beer, often with friends, passion-driven, grey conceptualization, hazy customer identity, funded with savings and hope, takes birth.

Chapter 2 – Yours to Reason Why!. 23

> Often driven by external factors, fuelled by peer pressures, hearsay and anecdotes, motivations driven by greed and desire, a know-it-all attitude, lead to early demises.

Chapter 3 – The Proof of Concept............37

Who is the customer, where do we find them, they see value in the idea, how can we reach him or her, who will deliver it, what will it cost us to deliver, what technology, what process, Skin in the game… the building blocks…

Chapter 4 – The First Days Out...............47

The rubber hits the road, compliances and complexities, low bank balances, no visibility to revenue or customers, sagging morale and tempo, no sounding board either.

Chapter 5 – Of Bootstraps & Garages..........61

Find a mentor, Focus on basics, Cash is a scarce commodity, under-hire and overdrive, grow teeth for the business, separate musts from wants, No business without revenues, constant reality checks…

Chapter 6 – The Outward View................71

Conscious focus on the market, talk extensively to customers, sample competitor offerings, continuous environment scanning, seek vendor and partner feedback, retain agility and speed to change, close the loop on customer complaints, ratify all assumptions, explore consulting opportunities.

Chapter 7 – Handcuffs & Shackles............83

Handicaps as challenges, the Credibility Gap, product and service offering perception, price and value connotations, Supplier and Partner skepticism,

Process lacunae, People and Quality challenges, Market Intelligence handicap, The Financial Squeeze.

Chapter 8 – The Fund-Raising Journey 97

Approach with caution, there are no free lunches, seek like-minded Investors, It's a journey, not the end, Stay Pragmatic and Honest, Promise only what is likely to be achieved, Carry your Co-Founders along, Appreciate the long term implications, Understand the small print, Seek guidance from mentors, find Financial expertise to enable the transaction, Documentation and Legal Paperwork is critical.

Chapter 9 – People & Team Building. 113

Look for enthusiasm and attitude, Hire fit-for-purpose, Open and Honest communication, Celebrate small wins, Engage beyond work, Share vision and objectives often, Recognize, Reward and share spoils, Hire to grow, Clarify Roles and Responsibilities frequently, Set benchmarks for Standards of performance, Lead by example, Use performance based compensation, Keep the Organization Lean, Integrity & Sharing Norms.

Chapter 10 – The Debt Deliberations 133

Not as easy as it seems, Sources and challenges, Costs and sacrifices, Bankers and their obsessions, The NBFC dilemma, Debt funds and Structured Debt, Trade-offs and implications, Payback and exits…

Chapter 11 – The Entrepreneurs' Realities 149

Too close to the action, a know-it-all syndrome, Bias for action overwhelms, perspective shortcomings, Playing hero or martyr, passion trumps rational thought, larger than the Enterprise, living only in the day, softer aspects take a back seat, Spreading too thin…

Chapter 12 – Generic Pitfalls to Avoid 165

The Idea Obsession, The Profitability Syndrome, The Here & Now Fallacy, All Battles have to be Won, The Cost Cutting Paradox, The Control Fixation, Benchmarking Against Giants, The Efficiency Mindset, The sunk cost conundrum, Stretch without Capability…

Chapter 13 – Concluding Thoughts. 187

Scaling up a venture is a Balancing Act, Strategy and Thinking Ahead is key, Process and People Investments a Must, Setting the Pace & Drive is a Given, Cash Flows Drive the Ability to Grow, Pricing and Credit Terms Critical, Vision and Hunger to Succeed are key ingredients, Regulations and Compliance need constant Watch, Teeth to Tail Ratios require Constant Calibration, Cash Breakeven an Essential Milestone, Personal Growth Must keep Pace…

Glossary of Terms and Phrases. 205

DEDICATION & ACKNOWLEDGEMENTS

This book is dedicated to the innumerable budding Founders, Promoters and Entrepreneurs, who have conceived, developed and built an idea into a possible business opportunity. Their obsessive passion, their relentless never-say-die attitude, their often young, inquisitive minds, with a thirst to acquire knowledge and business acumen, which has powered them to strive for success. Some of these whom I have seen, mentored, groomed and enabled hopefully, to better face and deal with the journey from a Start-up to a successful and profitable venture.

It is also dedicated to the growing ecosystem of Influencers, Investors, Advisors, Mentors and the like, who have committed to fuel the aspirations and expectations of these often starry-eyed and enthusiastic novices, to embark on this demanding journey on the road to creating a successful Enterprise. The Indian environment today, is testimony to their efforts, aided and abetted by favourable Government initiatives and support. May there be more of you, paving the way for creating an entrepreneur-driven economy!

My heartfelt gratitude to dear friends who shared thoughts, views and ideas often to aid and abet in my attempt to put it all together. A special shoutout to 'GR', the serial entrepreneur for his helpful feedback and suggestions, and Ulhas, the successful start-up stalwart, for his invaluable insights and profound thoughts, from his decade long journey to success.

Lastly, to my family, for allowing me to indulge in my need to express myself, and the space to pen this piece, in the middle of a pandemic driven lockdown. My son, for being the source of inspiration for me to get to work every day, without respite, by being a role model for commitment, passion, drive, creativity and application, which I am privy to, in his 'Work From Home' avatar! My wife, for being my sounding board, critic, support, motivator, and source of ideas and suggestions eternal! I am grateful for their presence and motivation!!

MESSAGE FROM THE SPONSOR

"SP-TBI has grown over the last few years due to symbiotic relationships developed with industry experts who have nurtured our start-ups. We were very clear on collaborating with experts who would be our guide and mentor. We found one such mentor in dear Mr. Raj Raman. He has been instrumental in supporting SP-TBI as a mentor. His role in assisting SP-TBI select start-ups for seed funds has been commendable too. We hope to grow further with his support and guidance."

– Dr. B.N. Chaudhari
Chairman, SP-TBI.

ABOUT SP-TBI

Sardar Patel Technology Business Incubator (SP-TBI) is an incubation centre founded in 2015 as an initiative of Bhartiya Vidya Bhavan's Sardar Patel Institute of Technology and is affiliated with the Department of Science and Technology, Government of India. Our objective is to cultivate entrepreneurship, promote innovation and support daring entrepreneurs. Our amenities include the best infrastructure, technology support, seed funding, talent pool, mentoring, training and much more. The SP-TBI supports technology start-ups from Education, Health, Energy, Agri-tech & IT Services. We also propose to extend our support to social enterprises making larger social impact and enterprises led by women entrepreneurs. Till date, we have successfully incubated 70 start-ups and created employment for over 750 professionals.

We invite applications. To apply:

Visit our Website: www.sptbi.com

Or Email us at: managertbi@spit.ac.in

Key programmes at SP-TBI

SP-TBI Incubation Programme.

SP-TBI Pre-Incubation Programme.

SP-TBI NIDHI Seed funding programme.

Firstpreneurs – Pwd Incubation Programme.

Salient Features:

- Separate Cabin in a plug and play office with 24X7 working hours facility.
- One to One Mentoring Support (Both Tech Mentor and Business Mentor).
- Access to Tech Lab and access to college labs at SP-IT.
- Access to Tech Talent.
- Opportunity to pitch before investors.
- NIDHI Seed support of up to Rupees 25 lacs.
- Industry Connections

PROLOGUE

*"Do not go where the path may lead,
go instead where there is no path, and leave a trail"*

– Ralph Waldo Emerson.

The Start-up ecosystem is a thriving, breathing, growing organism, fueled by the Millennial mindset, Covid constraints as an accelerator, Government and Education Institutions' focus and support, the robust Venture network, the Incubators, Consultants, Advisors and Mentors, leading and encouraging young budding brains to take the plunge. Often impulsive, off-the-cuff initiatives, the Start-up Ventures are slowly becoming a career option for the younger generation. We need to encourage and promote it, and that is a responsibility that we grey-haired oldies can take on, as we share our learnings and experiences, to guide them through the minefield of challenges and pitfalls.

Thus unfolded the genesis of the book. Extensive work in close proximity with the ecosystem and its components, has led me to believe that there are common and not-so-common errors which the budding entrepreneurs and founders make, which sets them off on the path to self-destruction and oblivion, unknowingly. Often the result of misplaced enthusiasm, they fall victim to the myriad seemingly unsurmountable challenges, that the journey of a start-up entails.

The effort here is to give a heads up on these pitfalls, and the ways of dealing with them, that are available to the Founders. Culled from the innumerable interactions, experiences, actions and fallouts one has seen over the past decade, these pointers and suggestions are just that. The Start-up environment remains as unpredictable, unimaginable, and totally challenging; the romance and excitement of the journey is often ignited by this, and is the key attraction for the souls who thrive in it.

All views, suggestions and thoughts expressed here are meant to better equip the farers of this journey to negotiate it with greater confidence, and not demoralize, discourage or deprive them of this unique experience. If it can contribute to improving the probability of success by a few percentage points, it can make a difference to a few thousands of Start-ups who have embarked on this journey. There are no 'one shoe fits all' solutions or strategies, nor is one trying to offer one. These are guidelines meant to make the thinking and execution process better, thus better positioning Founders and Entrepreneurs to cross the Rubicon, and emerge with a robust thriving business in the future!

Numerous success stories abound, often coloring perceptions and obfuscating associated realities. While studies of failures are few and far between, the insights they offer only reiterate the pitfalls highlighted in this narration. This is an attempt to precipitate thought, and highlight the pitfalls and challenges that litter the road to startup success.

Having said that, there is something exceptional about this Entrepreneurial journey. The high of having created a business out of an idea, made it work and the personal satisfaction and elation of becoming an independent, empowered and successful business person far outweighs any number of challenges and pitfalls one may encounter!

Here's to creating innumerable successful Enterprises, and an environment of innovation, application and appreciation and support, to the budding stars of the Start-up galaxy!!

Chapter 1

THE START-UP DNA

A germ of an idea, distilled with coffee and beer, often with friends, passion-driven, grey conceptualization, hazy customer identity, funded with savings and hope, takes birth.

A start-up in the classic sense, is little more than an idea, put together by a bunch of friends, and a culmination of a burst of high energy, over passionate exchanges and arguments, with a faint glimmer of a business at its core. Most of them are conceived in classrooms, dormitories, tea-shacks, coffee shops, favourite haunts, or simply on-the-fly.

The genesis of the theme evolves over innumerable cups of coffee/tea, some throwing together of opinions, a little flutter of a debate, a patchwork of thoughts, and lo and behold- here we are! A quick round of funds, through scraping together own savings, family contributions, is a 'quick and dirty' move in creating a start-up. The founders themselves are often, at best, hazy, on the value proposition, customer segment, market sizing and most other business parameters that one could think of.

The business plan, the core concept and its documentation follow, over many long sittings in coffee shops, meetings with associates, friends, well-wishers and so on, who all, invariably, bring in their own perspectives and thoughts, which are incorporated into the base document, as it evolves. During this period, adrenaline and passion keeps the founders on their toes, and helps them learn to live with anomalies, paradoxes, and dead-ends galore, which tend to creep into the plans and ideas.

There are no guidelines here; it's a bit of a trial and error, two steps forward and maybe even three backward, as baby steps are taken to bring the idea from the coffee table to the market, in the first instance. The offering continues to be shades of grey, the customer or segment continues to be everchanging, the differentiators with what already exists are yet to be mapped, and may not be significant, and the operational metrics, revenue and cost models, organization structure, delivery approaches, are nowhere near visualization, or faint existence.

There is then the mad scramble for getting things done; the offering design, the go-to-market approach, the search for execution partners, vendors, the cost angles and what they never thought of, the strong drive to somehow get it going, the tearing of hair over missing pieces, the brainstorming and quick fixes, the innumerable late nights and the search for answers where none exist. These are all inherent to the DNA of this animal we know, called a Start-up.

The environment plays its own role, and pandemics like Covid, create their own share of chaos; disruption begins even before the business can take a few baby steps. Salvage operations commence, some ideas are out of the window, some modified, some opportunistically changed, to push the idea towards becoming a germinating seed of a business.

How does this animal take birth, survive and finally thrive is a journey which consists of innumerable challenges and pitfalls; there are no standard solutions to make things right. The inherent DNA undergoes changes, twists, modifications, surgery and all possible interventions, before it qualifies as a venture which gets noticed. It's a long and treacherous road to the ultimate destination, a successful and growing business enterprise!

Strategies, tactics, interventions and methods-in-the-madness exist for all of this. The crux lies in the fact that it calls for a zero-base approach to the problem, often revisiting the inherent traits and gene strands of the basic DNA formed so far. Pointers to what they are, are often not seen by the Entrepreneurs and the Start-up crew; too close to the idea and action being the obvious reason. Uninvolved, unemotional assessments of the challenges often elude the Founders, their passion and love for their Venture often colouring and handicapping their ability to see the true picture.

All start-ups need to go through this cycle of conception, confusion, creativity, competency and commercial viability, before the idea reaches business dimensions. That journey, if undertaken with some time-tested guidelines, discipline and a strategic perspective, can help negotiate these pitfalls and challenges better. What these are and can be, comes by drawing upon the learnings and experiences of the hordes who have taken this journey earlier. It is my humble attempt to distil and present these as pointers, to enable the budding enthusiasts and their ventures improve upon the probability of becoming a successful Enterprise.

That precisely, it what is attempted here in the subsequent chapters, drawing upon the various interactions and experiences with Start-ups, early stage entrepreneurs, and their journeys, collected and refined over the past 10 years. The attempt is to present these, as though provokers, idea stimulators and a trigger mechanism to seek answers to some of the challenges.

Chapter 2

YOURS TO REASON WHY!

Often driven by external factors, fuelled by peer pressures, hearsay and anecdotes, motivations driven by greed and desire, a know-it-all attitude, lead to early demises.

I have had more than one passionate discussion with the promoters of start-ups, and the exchange would go something like this:

"Raj, we want to be the next Flipkart in India, and who knows, over time we will beat them!!"

"Why do you believe that?" I would counter.

"Our idea is better than theirs. They copied Amazon", Deepak, one of the founders, quips.

"Yours is an original? No one has attempted it before?" I probe.

"We have not checked, but we haven't heard of anything like it," is the reply.

"Didn't you Google it? I thought you guys were the whiz kids of the internet," I further encourage.

"We are way ahead of that. Our idea is out of the box, innovative and will be disruptive," Sachin the other founder counters.

"We are sure we will be able to become a unicorn and exit in 4 years; Flipkart and others have raised valuations multi-fold, and we can better that. Our objective is to be Billionaires in 5 years," is the triumphant riposte.

"There are so many of our friends and classmates, who have raised millions of dollars, with just an idea. We want to beat them, we had better CGPAs in the institute. With our efforts, we can beat them hollow," the argument continues.

"Anyway, the job scene is pathetic, and we don't need the paltry 30K to survive. We would rather make it on our own," a noble-intentioned quip comes back.

"My father can fund me and host me till then very easily," Deepak adds, with a triumphant glint in his eye.

"We believe customers will line up to use this app; the downloads and traffic will get us huge ad revenues," is Sachin's further contribution.

"You have done some customer testing and proof of concept? Glad to hear that," I encourage.

"No Raj. All that we will do later. We want to beat the team of Rashid and Uday, who are doing something similar, and started earlier. We got the thought from them. They are average guys. If they can do it, why can't we? The next adda we have, over beers, we want to announce our launch. We just need to talk to our dads for the 1 Crore we need for this."

"Do you really need that big an amount to start with?" I further probe.

"We have to open our office in the WeWorks BKC centre. We have already spoken to five members to join us, and we want our office space to be aspirational."

The story would go on for about 30 minutes or so, while coffee and cookies would materialize.

This team had reached out to me, referred by friends and well-wishers, as in most of these cases, as they wanted to get some guidance and ratification for what they had conceived and believed in. The concoction of coffee and bravado, was the elixir to pick my brains.

Sounds familiar? Unfortunately, the number of similar encounters that I have had, convinces me that there is a need for a serious speed-breaker and reality check for most of them. An early course correction and reflection, can go a very long way enabling a more balanced response, and dealing with the first set of challenges.

Let's examine the exchange a little more critically.

The Reasons Why Not To

1. **"Our Idea is better than Theirs!"** is a completely wrong approach and believing your idea to be unique, different and a winner, is the first pitfall of a number of start-ups I have seen. It's what is called a Confirmation Bias, or a 'my dogs are thoroughbreds' syndrome. The promoters and millennials who sometimes form part of the start-up crowd, tend to believe this more than others. They fall in love with their own idea to the point of becoming blind to obvious lacunae in their thinking. Blinded by this belief, the irony is that sometimes even reasonably good ideas, get into the cauldron of overconfidence, and what a little critical evaluation would have easily thrown up, is missed completely. The net result is a one-way ticket down the road of no return. Critical evaluation and dissection of the idea, and a strong "Devil's Advocate" approach to the process, can

most times prevent this unfortunate descent into oblivion.

2. **"We want to be the next Flipkart!"** is a dangerous rhetoric. It makes one drastically underestimate the ecosystem and its potentially disruptive events and ideas, while pushing one to a self-fulfilling prophecy of disaster of 'I am the best'. It's called the Survivors' Bias, as while one sees one successful venture and believes it's a piece of cake, one does not see the ones who failed, and are lost in oblivion. Rolf Dobelli, the author, calls for a "Visit to the cemeteries" to open ones' eyes and guard against this bias. Let's not forget that the road to success is littered with the bones of those who also-ran. For every icon we see, there are a thousand also-rans; the probability of success remains in basis points, or the rounding off errors!

3. **"Out of the box, Innovative and disruptive… our idea".** How often have we heard this, and yet the fallacy lies in the fact that every entrepreneur thinks his idea is the greatest. This fascination with the concept and business idea, is one of the major pitfalls for Founders. The propensity to get attached and obsessed with it, makes you blind to flaws often staring you in the face! The truth remains that successful Start-ups are rarely

totally disruptive and Innovative as a rule; such ventures are exceptions even in the ecosystem of the Start-up world. A little bit of pragmatism and a healthy 'devil's advocate' ethos, goes a long way in correcting any misconceptions that arise out of this, in the early stage. A good reality check is to actually bounce this off with people who are experienced, world-wise and disconnected with your business idea; they don't have anything to do with it. Don't make this self-aggrandization the basis of starting a venture… you are possibly setting yourself up for failure.

4. **"We want to be Billionaires in 5 years"** cannot be the sole reason to start the venture. Sure, founders do become billionaires, even earlier than 5 years, truth is, that is an outcome, and not the cause for the business. It can never be the core reason for starting a Venture. There has to be a value proposition which will meet unfulfilled needs of a customer, at its core. This pitfall is a serious handicap, as it works in many ways in guiding the thinking, efforts and goals of the venture, and thus creates a business on poor foundations. Don't let valuation be the end-game, the driver behind your idea. Do it because you believe in it; the investment, valuations, growth, success are all outcomes which

follow an intrinsically sound business idea and good execution.

5. **"So many of our friends and classmates have done this"** is another story one often hears, when we meet these budding entrepreneurs. A completely wrong reason to do this. 'Keeping up with the Joneses' is a sure ticket for disaster, and cannot be the foundation on which a venture is built. Don't do it because your friends did it and you were better than them in college; you don't know their story and journey, and each one of us has our own completely different and unique journey. Do it because you believe in it. Having said that, I still see a number of Start-ups coming to life as a typical herd reaction, driven by the immediate environment and the buzz in it. The 'dotcom' phase was one I recollect vividly. More recently I see a propensity to join the band wagon on Covid protection, healthcare and support systems. More often from people who are least equipped or driven to do so. Do it because you are passionate about it, not because your neighbour did it.

6. **"The job scene is pathetic and we don't need it to survive".** Maybe true, but don't use it as a reason to start a venture. I have had Start-ups

and promoters talking about this ad nauseum; a complete no-no as a basis of starting a venture. It is not and should not be the reason number one. If that becomes your approach, chances are, at the first opportunity of a good job, you will ditch your commitment to the idea and take up the job. Ask yourself if you like the idea of a start-up and running your own business. Speak to others who have embarked on this journey, get their first-hand experience and views, appreciate the realities and challenges of this adventure, before you jump into it. It's not everyone's cup of tea and may not be yours too!

A fallout of this, which I constantly experience is this whole rhetoric, that I have given up the opportunity to make a certain sum of money for 'X' years, and hence I should get adequately compensated by the valuation I create for my venture. This thought tends to consume the founders, at times distracting and disillusioning them. Have known a significant number of ventures who have missed the boat, because of this hangover.

7. **"My father can fund me"** is another unfortunate rhetoric often heard, in meetings and cafes. If that's the basis for starting a venture, your own

commitment and dedication to it, will follow the same thought process. You will see it as a 'time pass' or hobby, and not something you want to dedicate a significant portion of your life to. Hence, you would be setting yourself up for failure. Have often advised promoters to take a loan from the parent, and not equity, as it puts the additional responsibility of having to repay it, which works in aiding the start-up mind set. Parents in India, by and large, will gladly invest in their children's ventures, without batting an eyelid. But please do not exploit this as the crutch on which you build your business proposition and plans. A good business idea still needs to be the core driver of your plan.

8. **"We want to beat XYZ as we are better than them"** is a good motivator under certain circumstances, but cannot be the foundation of a business. There has to be a customer need, real or perceived, that you think you can fulfil, better than any existing player, either by way of product, or service, or cost, or value, or speed or convenience. Running your idea through this gauntlet, puts you in a much better position on the path to success. Your own perception of your capabilities vis-à-vis your peers, acquaintances,

relatives or friends, cannot become the reason you decide to start a venture. Apply the rationale of differentiation and value creation, as outlined earlier. Not a guarantee for success, but a good filter to use, to improve probability.

9. **"I did not get a job, so decided to…"** is another one I have heard. It's unfortunate but often tends to make founders end up starting sub-optimal business ventures, driven by desperation rather than inspiration. The emotional and psychological impact of this is telling on the energy, passion, commitment and determination that you approach it with. Not a very good path to take, and is often a set up for failure. The fact that you did not get a job, is an independent event; don't link it to your decision to have a start-up. For all you know, a few months down the line, you may be offered a job, which more than matches your expectations. Ask yourself whether you would still do this venture. Appreciate that your start-up has to be a stand-alone proposition and decision, not subject to preconditions or driven by circumstances.

10. **"ABC is willing to fund me, and I have X Dollars to burn"** only means that you are fulfilling someone else's dream. Make sure it is

yours to fulfil, else it will end up being another job clothed in venture duds. It often is a maze that you cannot exit out of easily. A few Founders I know, are struggling to deal with this reality, and often seek ways and means of resetting the button, in futility. Your expertise, knowledge or skills may be driving the funding decision, but make sure you have your heart in it, as otherwise you will end up being miserable. You may want to do something else, but you may be locked in contractually, which will prevent you from exiting this venture, to do so. This is a sure formula for aeons of misery. Tread lightly here.

11. **"I want to be my own boss…"** is a good thought, but don't make it the only reason for doing it. The fact remains that as the venture grows into a business, you will have Investors, Directors, a Board, Influencers, Employees, Customers, Regulators, who you will be either morally responsible for or accountable to. Following guidelines, caveats, laws, compliances, Board directives, become the norm with time. As your Venture grows and becomes successful, these will become prominent and significant, and you will need to operate within guidelines, and this may make you feel boxed in. Be pragmatic and accept this as a reality. There are

no free lunches; being coloured by today's distorted view, can lead to much misery later.

12. **"I have spent enough time in Corporate....I know this sector and business like the back of my hand"** is also something one hears, especially from seasoned professionals who take the plunge. Don't let this line of thinking be the driver of your decision to take the plunge. The truth tends to be a little different from this perception. The direct translation and application of the knowledge and experience does not happen, as the start-up environment requires its own set of adjustments, rethink, rejigs and often redesign, of what one has seen and experienced in the Corporate world. A good pragmatic reality check of all that one has learnt, and willingness to explore alternate views, approaches and experiences, is something that helps. It is prudent to guard against this syndrome of "I Know it all".

My advice to most start-ups, who seek some inputs and direction, has always been and is, *get the basics right*. A strong customer focus, environment scanning, competitor monitoring, core value proposition and differentiator, passionate and committed founders, healthy willingness and openness to learn, change and adapt, healthy respect for frugality, are essentials which puts the venture on a better footing, to launch yourselves towards success. However, there are no guarantees, and that uncertainty, is one of the attractions and adrenaline highs of journeying down this path!

Chapter 3

THE PROOF OF CONCEPT

Who is the customer, where do we find them, they see value in the idea, how can we reach him or her, who will deliver it, what will it cost us to deliver, what technology, what process, Skin in the game… the building blocks…

At the meeting of an Incubator's Investment Committee, the following conversation was heard:

"We think our concept will have great acceptance from the Indian consumer. We expect downloads to be 1 Million in the first year. The App is in the beta stage and ready," a proud Founding member of a Start-up proclaimed.

"What is the basis of your assumption? Have you done a survey and tested the app on potential consumers?" the senior-most member of the committee asked.

"We want to do that, but would first like to get some funding. It's going to cost money," came the hopeful response.

A quiet 30 seconds later "Have you at least done a pilot with some friends and family? I am sure you can do that at almost no cost," another member of the IC chipped in.

"We have so far spent all our time and money on developing the App. That is a quick job. We are sure we can complete it before the funding process is closed. We are only two of us, and our focus has been on getting this done." The line of conversation continued.

"We would like to see the Proof of Concept, if possible, before we consider the proposal," gently from the Committee Chairperson. "The whole business proposition rests on it, isn't it? What if there are no downloads, or there is no usage and activity post the downloads? Have you checked if there are similar apps already on Play Store?"

"We don't think anyone could have thought about this, as we haven't heard anything from our friends on this. Moreover, we want to launch it before anyone else does. Else we will miss the first-mover advantage" was the confident rhetoric.

"How is fulfilment going to happen? Who is doing it? Are you outsourcing that or do you have your own people for service?" the line of questioning by the IC continued.

"What is the cost of delivery of the service? Is the customer going to pay for the service? What is the revenue model? Who is paying for it?" another IC member questioned.

"We haven't done the costing, but plan to do the delivery ourselves. We have identified two boys for it. We will charge the customer a delivery charge of 200 rupees for each delivery," the founder member retorted.

"Your business plan shows a cost of 30 rupees per delivery, and a revenue of 500 Rupees per customer. Hope you have checked out the feasibility and costing, as well as the customers willingness to pay the price.", This from the senior-most member of the IC again.

The two gentlemen presenting, looked at each other and said "We estimated those numbers based on our gut feel. Once we get the funding, we will do a research and confirm," came the reply from the senior founder.

There was a moment of silence in the IC and then, "Thank you gentlemen. We will get back to you with our decision through the team here, in a day or two." The finality in the communication said it all.

Again, a feeling of Deja Vu? How often have we seen business plans with numbers off the bat, without a basis, or at least a reasonable guesstimate, made with certain assumptions? A closer analysis more often than not reveals that the attention to such details are missing in most plans put forth.

This is probably the first pitfall that most start-ups trip up on. A review of the conversation can be very illuminating here. Some pointers and red flags.

1. **Who is your customer?** A million downloads in year one, by itself is not alarming. What is, is the fact that you have not attempted to use secondary data, profiled your customer, sought their location, the numbers available to pick from for your profile, assumed a reasonable rate of conversion and hence the possible number of downloads. It takes just some amount of online research and a little number crunching, to arrive at a ballpark number for yourself. This cannot be wishful thinking or a number out of the hat. Unfortunately, the boys here have not even attempted to do that. Ventures

I have interacted with, sometimes tend to gloss over this, which is the cornerstone of any business plan you make.

2. **Where can we find them?** A basic study of a sample, and then an extrapolation will also do. But any numbers we throw have to have some foundation and background, and its assumptions. Some of the things the IC discussed later, were the location and geography of the distribution of this potential customer base, and their ability to reach them. The concern unanimously was the lack of application to get to the bottom of this, which demonstrated a certain bravado minus substance. Consequently, there was agreement that they are also likely to not tax their intelligence to figure out ways to reach them, efficiently and economically. In reality, they may have had the foresight and guidance to actually do so, but this was the perception created, and hence a missed opportunity for the duo.

3. **Funding First and then POC?** Often the rhetoric one hears with ventures just taking shape. That's putting the cart before the horse, to put it bluntly. Forget the Investors or Incubators, won't you at least satisfy yourself that you do have a working concept? Be it naivete or arrogance, whatever drives

such behaviour is a pitfall you can and should do without. A proof of concept is a must, before we can go to a funder, even if they are incubators. A question I often ask Founders of Start-ups is, 'If it was your own funding, would you go ahead without doing a Proof of Concept?' Invariably, I see embarrassed faces, grinning sheepishly and doing a quick exit, presumably to get back to the drawing board.

4. **"Focussed on the App first, only two of us…"** Naïve approach to believe that funding will happen first, and then we can get into the nitty-gritties of execution and pilots. There has to be a basis for confidence in the idea, and at least an informal focus group amongst friends; this is the least expected, before you go out into the world to seek funds. It is a very common malaise, often the result of reluctance to seek ratification of the idea and staying in their own comfort zones, by the founders. It's important to execute a full cycle, which will throw up a number of surprises, and expose shortcomings of the idea, as a business. Successful ventures are not built on untested and unvindicated hypotheses.

5. **Obsessive Arrogance and No Environment Scanning.** "We believe no one else has thought

of it…want to have the first mover advantage." A few buzzwords and concepts stay with the Entrepreneurs and the first mover advantage is one of them. Possibly something they heard in their gatherings or from friends and acquaintances. It is a foregone conclusion that if you succumb to this 'perception based intellectual arrogance' of shoot-ready-aim, you have probably fallen into the biggest pit at this stage! More often than not, such arrogance and the desire to be there first, makes most Start-ups do a half-baked launch, and shoot themselves in the foot. Make sure you don't join that gang, please!

6. **The Fulfilment Challenge.** If there is one common thread one sees across Start-ups struggling to make things happen, it is this operational capability and think-through. It is considered unglamorous and painstaking, and is hence relegated to the bottom of the areas of focus and priorities. The truth, though unpalatable, is the fact that even an average business idea, executed well, has a better chance of making it as a venture, than the most brilliant one, where the execution nitty-gritties have been relegated to the minions by the founders. Unfortunately, the chain is only as strong as the weakest link. It often

blows up in your faces. Please desist and be wary of this pitfall!

7. **Simplistic Solutions for Delivery and Fulfilment.** "we will do it ourselves." With two Founders and no one else! As ridiculous as it sounds, it's heard once too often from these young Entrepreneurs. The largest time and incessant efforts need to be devoted to getting this equation right. The grunt work, as it is perceived, is what ensures the model is workable, and allows you to then figure out the costs associated with doing it. To complicate things further, it remains a dynamic and constantly changing animal, influenced by legal and procedural changes, competitor approaches, geographical anomalies, or Covid like factors!

8. **"We have not costed it in detail but the customer will be charged X…"** The mistake most often made, is to think you can charge your customer what you think is right, or what is costs you, plus a profit. Unfortunately, this thought is completely divergent from the reality. Business plans are drawn up, with cost and revenue projections based on internal compulsions, which is the reality in most cases. The fact of the matter is, that these

factors, i.e. costs and price, both are driven by market forces and realities. A customer will pay only what he perceives as the value of the product or service, and the costs will be driven by what the market rates for such services are. There are no short-cuts!!

9. **"We will do POC and research once funding comes in…"** is another red flag for most external funders and investors. It is critical that you are able to demonstrate your commitment to the idea and business, by way of self-funding as seed capital. It is an indication of your own 'skin in the game' as Founders. Boot strapping, and putting together your own savings, with friends and family contributions to create a small corpus to begin with, gives comfort to potential supporters, influencers, investors and even incubators.

Promoters and Founders of Start-ups need a reality check on the market-driven home truths than anything else. The absence of this exposure is often the result of the fact that our education system fills them with theories and constructs of Technology, Engineering, and other subjects, but exposure to business creation, market dynamics and its nuances, are often limited, or totally missing!! Take a deep-dive, and do the think-through on this, early on. It provides a foundation which then allows for ambitious risk taking and speed in execution.

Chapter 4

THE FIRST DAYS OUT

The rubber hits the road, compliances and complexities, low bank balances, no visibility to revenue or customers, sagging morale and tempo, no sounding board either.

"Sir, we need a few hours of your time." These were opening lines from Raghavan and his partner, Sam, on a conference call with me. The two were first time Entrepreneurs and Founders of a start-up in the consumer space. I had been requested by a friend to handhold them, and hopefully, to better ensure their chances of success.

"Sure, Rags. Any fires? Hope all moving well with your Venture," I respond, with a view to break the ice, and give them an opening.

"We are facing serious challenges, and don't know who to speak to," Sam volunteered. "We have not done any of this before and don't know how to go about it" he continued.

"Can we see you today if possible?" said Rags, with a note of desperation and a hint of despair in his voice.

"Let's try and catch up late in the evening, as that is the open slot when I can meet you" I said, not wanting to disappoint them, and with an objective of giving them encouragement and empathy.

"We also need to show you something… We need to find answers quickly," Sam quickly chipped in.

"Look forward to hearing you out to understand your challenges… see you soon." I could sense their angst and concern, and had a possible thought on what could be the underlying factors.

A conversation which is very often played out, in coffee shops, restaurants, offices, hotel lobbies, on zoom, on telephone, with varying shades of despair, depression, dejection, gloom or frustration.

May not appear very familiar at first, but the story line that unfolds is very often one with eerie similarities across businesses, industries or verticals. Getting under the skin of these terse comments, as we peel the onion, we unravel the mystery. The truth then starts to dawn on all of us.

My meeting with the team of Rags and Sam, who were doing a Fast Moving Consumer Goods (FMCG or CPG) start up, revealed an early wave of challenges that most of them encounter. The pattern remains more or less the same as the rubber hits the road…

1. **The first month syndrome.** The venture starts to feel like a drudgery, as the first month plays out. Progress is scarce, too many roadblocks and challenges to getting things moving, new data and compliances to deal with, and many more. It is confusing, frustrating, and often daunting in appearance to most of the newbies and young Founders, for whom it is a first in many ways. Just the plethora of new angles, perspectives, activities, decisions, and information to deal with, is often overwhelming. A reality check and understanding that these are not as radical and impossible challenges to encounter, and a few pointers on dealing with it enables one to compose oneself, and move ahead with more confidence. Forewarning and preparedness for this, works to your advantage. It enables you to brace yourself and be prepared for the chaos and onslaught that is coming at you! Raghavan and Sam had wilted under it.

2. **The Compliances and Legalese.** Company formation, registrations, and documentation is another set of challenges for Founders of these ventures. Never exposed, it can appear to be unsurmountable, and the numerous opinions and suggestions from well-wishers will only frustrate one further. Get a good Chartered Accountant and Company Secretary to help with all of this. He or she will be able to guide, and help execute the myriad pieces of compliance one needs to navigate through. These should be right on top of your priorities. Any lacunae here, will mean long term damage to reputation, credibility and the ability to build stature. Have often had to intervene and guide some of the Promoters, who reach out, especially when due diligence is being done by a potential Investor, in the first instance. The expense as it is, upfront, is a non-negotiable, and will be more than worth it. The downside to ignoring this, will come back to haunt you later in the journey, with both costs, barriers and heartaches, multi-fold.

3. **The Lack of Infrastructure.** Raghavan and Sam were reeling under the chaotic lack of workspace and infrastructure. Coffee shops, own homes, street corner shanties, mall food courts and even

hotel lobbies, were not ideal places for discussions or interviews for hiring. To top it all, the need for an office address was now beginning to bite them, and they were unsure where they could start. Their entire conversation was on seeking options to deal with this conundrum. Not an easy problem to solve - though Incubators, shared offices, co-working spaces offer some solutions, the cost structures appear daunting most times. Pay-per-hour is also a serious option, as they do provide an address for the office, and the infrastructure headaches are not yours to deal with. It may not be obvious, but a smart search can give you a shared office space, that may be worth the thought and more. The invisible costs, sometimes are not appreciated till you have to do so yourselves. A thumb rule of 1.8 to 2 times the quoted rent will be your actual cost, considering these. Cost apart, the air conditioning, electricity, security, housekeeping, drinking water, restrooms and pantry are not something you then need to look into, which is a big relief! It allows one to focus on the business building blocks.

4. **The Cash Crunch.** Most times, the stress on cash availability only begins to bite, as the spends mount. Infrastructure, compliance, banking,

people and technology, start biting into the reserves which we think we have plenty of, to begin with. In a few months, what appeared to be a good long runway to take off, suddenly looks like a helipad on a hilltop. The fall appears imminent, and the source of additional cash, non-existent. Revenues are not visible, and you see the drain on the bank account and cash every day. Sam's concern was that there was not enough to see them through 6 months, at current rate of spends. A very pragmatic look at what one was spending on, a budget to begin with, a tracking and monitoring of the spends, gives one the feeling of being in control, and helps one breathe much easier. The best solution to avoid this, is to get the budgeting done upfront, and follow it to a T, with no exceptions. Both Raghavan and Sam were relieved and grateful for the quick budget we could draw up for them to follow and monitor, at least for the time ahead!

5. **Identifying Suppliers and Service Providers.** This often-ignored area creates long term weaknesses in the entire journey as you build the business. A few days of extra effort, in identifying the best there is, and engaging over a slightly longer time frame, to get to know, align and educate them on your

business objectives, is worth its weight in gold. While ensuring service standards and good price points, this helps in creating a strong foundation for a long association. The premise to work with is that you are here to create a perpetual business. The best sources for all these are suppliers to competitors, similar businesses, common supply chains, customer references, recognition & awards, memberships of associations, to begin with. Online searches can throw up a reasonable short list, and helps one get started. Employees who come from the Industry or have experience in other Organizations can also be good sources of a short list. A connect through a common acquaintance or friend, is worth its weight in gold, as you sift through these. References and introductions, go a long way in cementing good ties.

6. **Hiring the first few employees.** The key to creating a good and robust business is to ensure you hire the right people to begin with. While everyone is critical, the first few are like the foundations for the edifice of a quality organization. It is not easy. In the absence of an office, a business, awareness and reputation, in some cases even a website, it is purely a personal charisma, sell and evaluation that can make someone join you. Don't throw money

to do it. Often the wrong move, as individuals who are driven by money tend to look at large moneyed and funded Ventures as their goal, and hence you will end up being a stepping stone, an interim option till a better one comes along, and be a training and experience centre for them. The paradox of this whole process is that the real good potential employees, will be hesitant, and the ones who are eager and willing, may be a compromise for you. Strike a balance. As the venture blooms, you will have the luxury of upping the standards, while at the same time, giving the early few the opportunity to come up the curve, and grow into great employees and team members. This 'Good to Great' transition can be a win-win for both.

7. **Basic Processes and Review.** Raghavan was struggling with not being able to instil the sense of urgency, or a passion in what the rest of the team members were doing, and often found time was being wasted in loitering or surfing the net. Sam and he were finding it difficult to monitor everything, while keeping an eye on the ball, and getting the critical building blocks in place. My advice to anyone struggling with this is, communicate your Vision and Goals and make them visible, define objectives and roles for all, create a daily

checklist, a morning stand up meeting and review schedule, delegate within predefined boundaries, and keep updating and dynamically revising roles, objectives, goals and daily lists as you go along. A team works best when they know what is the Goal they are chasing, the steps and milestones and their own roles in the journey. Passion and commitment are generated only when we have a clear understanding of where we fit in in any team and its ultimate goal. Constant evaluation and visible progress are also stepping stones to creating a driven team. Don't worry about the list of deliverables being comprehensive or complete. A rudimentary one will do. Get effective first, then look for efficiency!!

8. **Business process definition and standards.** Early in the venture, is the time to define what you want to do, how it will be delivered to the customer, and identify technology and processes that will be needed to do it. A basic flow, with inputs, outputs and deliverables is a good starting point. As the business grows and scales, the flow will need to be dynamically updated, changed or modified, as in various stages of the Organization, the inputs, deliverables and standards change, often driven by business complexities and market dynamics. Both

Sam and Raghavan were seeking this help too, when they met up. One of the benefits of doing this, is it helps bring all employees up to speed and on the same page, which they realised once this was put in place. In a growing enterprise with multiple locations and remote working, it becomes mandatory. Working From Home, or 'WFH' as we have all quickly got used to, makes it even more crucial to have these in place, for synergistic working and execution.

9. **Organization processes and documentation.** Define simple rules and protocol for how the venture as a Company will work. Timings, leave, compensation and salary-slips, work ethics and discipline, expenses and claims, dos and don'ts at a basic level, all enable a stable and reasonably working venture. In WFH times, where a formal personal induction is a remote possibility, these act as guidelines and make the new employees get comfort and a feeling of belonging to a particular enterprise. It may appear foolish, and stupid to begin with, but is again a basic tenet of creating a sustainable Organization. Standard forms, formats and templates for letters, logos, cards, messages, voice recordings, all help in not only creating an Organizational identity, but also slowly create a

sense of pride and ownership amongst the other members of the Venture.

10. **Communication.** Often not understood and rarely appreciated is the need to communicate with employees, suppliers and customers on an ongoing basis. Creating a process for doing so, and speaking the same language and giving the same messages, were the two key aspects which I gently reiterated and emphasized to the duo. As founders and leaders of the venture, it is a primary responsibility of yours, to keep constantly reminding everyone concerned, about what the Venture is all about, its objectives, its philosophy, its long and short-term goals, its values and beliefs, and what it stands for. You personally, will have to first buy into all of this, before you will be able to communicate this with conviction and sincerity. It goes a long way in keeping people involved, motivated, passionate, and building a comfort and trust in the founders and promoters.

11. **Founders Roles and Responsibilities.** It is probably the most critical of the rules of engagement and work, as it often tends to become a challenge as the Organization grows and complexities creep in. Clearly define which founder will drive which aspect of the business

early, and respect and honour what is agreed upfront. It helps manage the Organization and team better, and is a good foundation for a well-run business. Define the decision-making process with authority and delegation, allowing the Founder driving the aspect, to take calls and move ahead. A conflict resolution process too, between Founders is a must, as it helps make the day to day working smooth and seamless. As Founders, your cohesive and seamless efforts are what will drive the success of the Organization!

All of this, was what was bothering the two gentlemen, but they were not able to put their fingers on it. The two hours spent in giving them a direction and set of objectives for the next few months, gave me a quiet sense of satisfaction as I could see it had worked. By the time we left, they were both looking much more relaxed, smiling, and appeared far more confident in being able to deal with the chaos around them. My earnest suggestion to all you budding Entrepreneurs will be, please devote time and attention to these aspects, which I have chosen to highlight above. These are really methods and pointers to navigate the pitfalls and prepare yourself for the other challenges ahead.

The first few months are the most difficult for any start up. All of the above, in varying degrees and hues, come up and confront the promoters. Being able to identify them, deal with them, and create workable solutions to handle them, will go a long way in allowing you the critical time and bandwidth to focus on the other even more critical aspect of building the business, and addressing the customer and the market side of things.

Chapter 5

OF BOOTSTRAPS & GARAGES

Find a mentor, Focus on basics, Cash is a scarce commodity, under-hire and overdrive, grow teeth for the business, separate musts from wants, No business without revenues, constant reality checks...

Anu and Jaya were both sharing a quick cup of coffee. A routine that had been solidified over the past few months, it helped them exchange quick ideas and charge each other up, before the challenging day ahead.

"There is so much we have to accomplish, and time is scarce" Anu complained.

"I think we are trying to do too many things at the same time" Jaya retorted.

"That is always the case in the early days, isn't it? It is important we are able to get things moving on various fronts. The first customer, the process standardization, people to deliver, identifying new prospects, fixing our infrastructure, paying our suppliers and vendors, getting the price equation right, finalizing the packaging design and production, finalising distributor agreements, are all on the table." Anu as the CEO, rattled off the list.

"We also have our employees to motivate, our budgets to stick to, ensure discipline in office, find replacements for people who exit, reallocate their work, resolve customer complaints, get our office décor fixed, get the visiting cards and stationery finalized, get the call centre up and running…" Jaya, the COO continued.

"How do we get all of this done? We need at least 3 more people in the team" with a touch of exasperation in her voice.

"We cannot afford anymore till we start showing some revenues and cash inflow" Anu opined. "We have been over this before, haven't we?"

"Aren't we being a little penny-wise pound foolish? If we do not invest today, we cannot grow," was Jaya's opinion.

"We have to make do. Our cash availability only gives us 6 months, on today's run rate of expenses. Anything more, and we may have to shut shop earlier."

"We will have to prioritize and make our spends. How much of it is what we actually need and how much is just our wish list? Let's talk to our mentor to see if there is a way out. Let's do a coffee with Rajat this evening?" Anu suggested before she moved towards the door.

A typical exchange in most start-ups in the early days, between founders. Swamped with a checklist running into pages for each day, it is critical Anu and Jaya, whose Children's Garments start-up was slowly taking its final shape, arrive at a common ground of what to push for, and what to shelve or kill, if they are to make it through the next 6 months.

Often this conundrum, tends to stymie the Founders and Promoters, and an unbiased perspective helps resolve issues. Some pointers for those confusing and confounding days, which could help deal with them better.

1. **Find a Mentor early**. One of the challenges of venturing to put together a business from an idea, is the devastating bombardment of decisions and actions that appear out of nowhere and need to be done immediately, leaving one completely lost and bewildered. The challenge becomes a constant battle between short and long term, urgent and

important, musts and needs, business development versus delivery, investments and expenses, inward actions versus market plays, and so on. To top it all, your own limited ability and knowledge of these to understand, anticipate and appreciate them, stymies and handicaps your ability to negotiate and deal with them appropriately. Being too close to the action often results in differing points of view, coloured by the proximity to the challenge. This pitfall is a no-brainer and a given for most companies in the early stages. It is important that founders find a mentor, coach and advisor, with rich and diverse experience, and worldly wisdom, who will help them navigate this tricky minefield, early in their journey.

The individual who fits these shoes should be someone with more experience that the founders, whom they all respect. worldly-wise and a good thinker, who has spent adequate time and navigated the corporate maze before, with an ability to maintain a detached and distanced view, enabling him or her to have a complete perspective of the potential idea and the emerging business. Someone who can direct and course-correct the Founders, using all of this, to guide them to doing what is most appropriate in the situation. A good shoulder to cry on too, if need be, but definitely a person to go to, for reality checks and course-corrections.

2. **Focus on the basics.** A good approach to some of these decisions is always to ask oneself, if the importance of the decision is basic and crucial to the tenets of the business. Is it an essential building block and core to the potential business? If the answer is yes, then the priority to this should be higher than anything else. Easier said than done though, and often the help of a good mentor is needed to resolve this. A good way of checking it out would be to ask yourself if the customer will be willing to pay a price for whatever you want to invest or spend on. The temptation to go the whole nine yards, and pull out all the stops for the business, is a big deterrent and barrier, and a constant reality check of whether it is a 'must' or a 'nice to have' is called for.

3. **Cash is a Scarce Commodity.** It's not called bootstrapping without a reason. The early days will always be a period where you will be perpetually short in the bank. The need will remain significantly above the availability and the prudent use of this scarce commodity, cash, will ensure the business gets the runway it needs

to start showing signs of materializing from the potential. A ruthless 'No' to anything that does not further the business, is a must. Luxuries like a wonderful office, branded furniture, top-of-the-line laptops, and other topline amenities can all wait. Hard negotiations for price and credit terms, tough cuts and pull backs, setting a minimum benchmark for products and services to buy, are all par for the course. Survive and create, before you thrive and grow! A throwback to getting to be effective first.

4. **Must Haves versus Needs.** Cash conservation measures do get you going on this, but worth treating it as a separate initiative too! A key factor to drive such decisions and spends should also be a hard look at what is essential to the business, and what is actually our own need to have or a desire. Keep doing this check, as the propensity to mistake our own desires for a business must, is very high, especially in the early stages. Ask yourselves a number of times before you commit to the spend or investment, as they are often not recoverable or reversible. A good method of doing this is to arrive at a list of what you will not spend money on, early, before you commence or commit to any spending. A budgeting exercise is a useful

tool in this regard. Else 'Water under the bridge' can leave you with regrets for a long time to come.

5. **Hire like a Miser.** One area that we all need to closely watch and ruthlessly adhere to with an audit-like scrutiny, is the need to hire, the corresponding cost of the hire and its long-term implications. You will always be short of an ideal budget and a licence to hire. Hiring beyond minimum required numbers, a more expensive resource, a more qualified and experienced one, are all errors which can have long term implications. One useful pointer to keep in mind is that always hire one if you think you need two people. See the benefit and progress, and defer the next hire till it begins to pay off, in terms of value addition to the organization. A bad hire or excessive hire at this stage, can push the venture back by months, if not years, leave alone the heartburn and discomfort of the entire process.

6. **Get Teeth in Early.** There can be no business venture without customers, and to get them you need focus on this critical activity of searching, finding, identifying, and converting potential to actual ones. Early-stage ventures find this one of the biggest pitfalls they encounter. Get your front end, business engine manned, to start with. These

are the people who will acquire the customers and get you the business. Goes without saying that in all cases, the CEO has to lead from the front, and in B to B enterprises, should hold fort till the first few customers are on board. In most cases, this is the most difficult thing to do in terms of hiring or decisioning, as it's possibly the truest test of the business model and its value proposition. If you cannot acquire customers, then it's a farewell to the Venture. The founders and promoters should themselves be involved in this, more than anything else, with the CEO designate making it his or her core deliverable, upfront.

The business requires 'teeth', which is another word for the frontline individuals, whose core task is to ensure customers are acquired to get things going. I have often seen start-ups, with a 15-member team, but none dedicated to acquiring the customer, who is the reason for existence of the business! Make sure your hiring focus remains fixed on this, and evaluate every position relative to this criticality. In a crunch, would prefer you hire the teeth, to someone to do the backend. Having more customers to serve, is a better problem to have, than have more in the backroom, waiting for the customers to show! In a trade off, would look to strengthen the engine of the Company.

7. **No Business without Revenues.** Most of us, in our eagerness to get off the blocks, tend to think that once we have a customer, we have crossed the Rubicon. Not true! What is a must, is a paying customer, and the venture needs to clock in revenues from customer acquisitions, not just 'pro bono' customers per-se. It is a ratification and validation of our business idea, the assumptions we have made, the value proposition and the processes we have put together, for the idea to see light of day! It is a monumental step in the journey towards building a successful business, and needs to be right up there on the priority list. This endorsement has immense positive fallouts and ramifications. Not only does it act as an elixir, and motivates and encourages us as founders, it works as a huge plus for employees, potential investors, partners and well-wishers as well! The credibility, belief and confidence in the Venture and you as Promoters, makes a significant, quantum leap!

8. **Let Energy and Enthusiasm loose.** This period of high stress, multitasking, team building, norms establishment, new relationships, working partnerships and customer acquisition, calls for

the ability to consciously unwind and keep the Venture from spiralling into chaos. Accept and love the chaos, encourage and cheer all around you, and keep your own motivation consciously high. A tough ask, but critical to cement and bind the newly forming team together. Have seen the impact of not doing this, and it tends to take away from all the other gains one has made in the journey thus far. Don't miss out on this, I cannot emphasize this more! It will go a long way in carrying everyone through the struggles and trying periods ahead, which is bound to be there in our journey. There is more to come, and a good spirited and cheerful team, is a big plus for it.

These are diverse challenges and pitfalls, with pointers to deal with, and may seem totally unrelated, but often rear their heads at the same stage in the journey. These challenges are very typical of bootstrapping days, and dealing with them effectively goes a long way in keeping the venture humming and ticking. Preparing and dealing with them effectively, is a big bonus and earns you the luxury of more time, better cash comfort, a motivated and energised team, and most importantly, puts you personally, in a better position and mind space, to look forward to the next stages of this journey.

Chapter 6

THE OUTWARD VIEW

Conscious focus on the market, talk extensively to customers, sample competitor offerings, continuous environment scanning, seek vendor and partner feedback, retain agility and speed to change, close the loop on customer complaints, ratify all assumptions, explore consulting opportunities.

The mentoring discussions were animated and vociferous. Sajid and his partner, Ramnik were picking my brains for their Venture, where things had started to unwind, according to them.

"There is no traction on the product and our offering" Ramnik voiced, with dejected finality.

"We haven't given it long enough to say anything conclusively" Sajid countered.

"We have been at it for 3 months now, and I don't see any customer either buying our product, or even willing to talk."

Ramnik and Sajid had a Cyber security venture, which they had conceived and designed, and were passionately committed to.

"We have not done enough of potential customer presentations and interactions. Our efforts need to be better and more focussed "Sajid opined.

"But we have been trying to get meetings with key influencers and decision makers, and that takes time," Ramnik countered.

I had been watching the exchange of words and repartees with interest, and decided to intervene at this stage.

"How many presentations have you made so far? How many influencers and decision makers have you been able to meet? "was my first question.

"I am sure most Banks and Financial institutions you have met would be using some form of cyber security. Am I right? Do you have an idea of what they are using? Any data or information? "was my second question.

"What are the pain points of what they are experiencing today? Sajid, you know most Chief

Technology Officers in the banks. Have you tried picking their brains for this?"

My line of questioning I could see was getting them both to pause and reflect. Ramnik and Sajid looked at each other, and chorused, "Sir, please elaborate a little on this."

I then spent the next 30 minutes or so, giving them a few pointers on what might work better.

Nothing very mystical about it. Most Start-ups encounter this dilemma at some stage in their early days. Converting an idea and the hypothesis of the product's utility and value, into business, calls for actually looking at it from the customer's point of view. Seek opinions, pain points, feedback, and use that to fine tune the offering to fit into the opportunities that you thus identify.

It's the cornerstone of the business, and calls for serious outward viewing and scanning the environment, to get this right. Everything else, then tends to fall in place.

Some pointers to keep in mind, and execute.

1. **Focus on the Market Consciously.** Make sure, in the early days, you consciously bring yourself to focus on the market for a fair period of time. Often, I have found that Promoters and Co-

founders tend to get too caught up in the chaos of the basics, as outlined earlier, and tend to remain inward looking. It takes away from vital market and customer facing time, crucial to get things going from a business point of view. All the inward attention is not going to help, if the effort is not taken to seek the market view on your product or service idea. You have to force yourself away from the innumerable in-house challenges to look at this consciously. Set aside time every day for doing this, irrespective of the prevalent chaos, fires and demands on your time. It is also a fact that this is something which is new to you, as first-time entrepreneurs and hence, needs an additional push, for you to get out of your comfort zone, and explore.

While the roles and responsibilities you have allocated to yourselves as founders, may mean one of you is predominantly inward focussed, and the other outward, it is important to deliberately switch at times and do the reverse, even for a day, to get a better perspective of things.

2. **Talk to Potential Customers.** Not easy, but is a pre requisite to getting the business off to a start. B to C business ideas are easier in this regard, but the number of potential customers you speak

to, needs to be significantly higher as a sample size. On the other hand, in B to B businesses, it necessitates that you establish and identify sources or connects, to give you the time and introductions to people who could be influencers, or decision makers, and fairly knowledgeable about the area of focus of your Venture. These approaches will unearth valuable information on the pain points and business needs, with gaps that exist in current offerings. You will be pleasantly surprised at the plethora of information, and quality of the pointers you get, to finalize your pitch, fine-tune your offering, and structure your commercials or pricing, as you go along this journey of converting the idea to a product or service of value. It is a very essential step in your journey to fruition of your dreams and aspirations. Please take the time and trouble to do this; it will save your venture from blindly careening down a path, which could possibly only end one way, disastrously!

3. **Check Competitors' Products and Services.** One of the ways of keeping tabs on the competition which is used fairly well by smart entrepreneurs, is to order a product or service of the competitor and experience the cycle of purchase, the product, and the standards of

service. A demonstration or presentation is even better, but difficult to manage possibly. It works as a very good benchmark to map against your own offering and structure your pitch, literature, to highlight the plusses you bring to the table. If there are no direct comparable products, check out similar offerings in the same domain, and to the same customer segment. If a bank, check similar products or services being offered to them, and the service levels and delivery standards they meet. Benchmarking and constantly evaluating your own against the others, is a sure way to keep your business ahead of the curve, in a competitive and dynamic environment. Stay on top of innovations and changes from competition as that will impact your business.

4. **Environmental Scanning.** The outward view is incomplete without a process of scanning the environment for tweaks and changes in innovations, regulations, customer preferences, disruptive products and services, and not just competitor activity. Secondary research on the net, a huge benefit of digitization, is possibly the bare minimum that one needs to do. Not only in your own defined market at present, but it is equally important to scan the larger global market

too, as pointers on what could be on the horizon, is a distinct possibility. Disruptive technologies, processes and operating methods, can easily derail and undo all the progress you could have made in a jiffy! Other ways of completing this scan exist too. Industry gatherings, seminars, literature and research papers, knowledge sharing and best-practice sessions can all be potential sources of intelligence gathering. Your focus needs to be to keep looking for such opportunities to get a better perspective on what the environment and its changes portend, for your Venture.

5. **Talk to Partners, Suppliers and other Intermediaries.** While your Venture could be a fledging in the business and market, the partners, suppliers and other intermediaries have been around for a while in most cases. Hence, their information and knowledge base, should be a very important source of data gathering - on the industry, market, competition, changes and innovations in products and services as well as pointers for changes in consumer behaviour. Often neglected, these valuable sources of nuggets of crucial insights, can more often than not, make a significant difference. I know of Organizations which make this a practice, and have benefitted

immensely in their journey of scaling the business. On a different note, they are also useful for identifying good potential employees, technology partners, investors and connects in Government. Do spend time in consciously cultivating this informal network.

6. **Retain Agility and Speed to Change.** All the above is useless if you do not cultivate a culture of agility, flexibility and speed of response, to stimuli thus gathered. It may mean tweaking the pricing strategy, the process of delivery or pivoting the go-to-market approach, to account for the unforeseen changes and impact of those. Don't get bogged down by the fact that you have finalised your offering and service, and need to be wedded to it. A good process would be to keep a weekly session to discuss this exclusively, and work out your response to anything which is out of the ordinary in all the information gathering for the week. Else, it remains a useful tool for bringing everyone up to speed on the outward view. Knowledge of the industry and business is a requisite in today's digitized and quick changing world, and ensuring all employees are up to speed, goes a long way in building a cohesive, smart and functionally effective business unit.

7. **Track and Resolve all Customer Complaints.** Again, an often, underrated activity, but in a digitally connected marketplace, is a very powerful tool and intervention, to gain goodwill and brand salience. 'Word of mouth' and a viral messaging often does more than what expensive marketing dollars do for you. But it cuts both ways, and a good service recovery, can be a major plus, while the possible downside losses, you cannot afford as a start-up. So, create a conscious culture of listening and noting down all issues, pointers, suggestions that come through from your first set of customers. They're often the more adventurous risk takers, early adapters, and are also likely to be the most active in terms of networking and sharing across forums and groups. Opinion makers like them, can make or mar the future of your company and business. Work smart around this reality. Use this to your advantage, as you start to build a franchise for your Enterprise.

8. **Reassess all Assumptions Continuously.** Analyse and dissect all feedback and information that you are constantly gathering, and evaluate all your earlier business, product, service and customer assumptions against this. Make changes on the fly, if there are serious areas of concern, and changes

that need to be done! Bite the bullet, swallow pride, and change! These early days, are a period of constant tweaking, redesigning, refactoring, redefining all aspects of the product and its service components. Make that a mantra, as it will take a few quarters or even years of doing this, before you can get a firm handle on the specifications that matter and deliver standards that excel. It is worth its weight in gold, so to speak. A robust process and culture of doing so, will allow you to stay ahead of the curve, as the market for the offering of yours, grows, stabilizes and enables you and the team to deal with everything from competitive product challenges to disruptive alternatives.

9. **Explore Consulting or Evaluation Opportunities.** As Founders, if your expertise is domain knowledge and experience, seeking opportunities for Consulting or Evaluation of projects, may actually open doors and, over time, translate into potential long-term customers for your business. It creates an opportunity for you as well to keep tabs on the latest happenings and processes in the industry, while gaining access to industry practitioners and practices, real time. Additionally, it helps you get a close-up view of

real issues and challenges in the industry, and may enable and guide improvements in your own product or service offerings to address those, or identify new opportunities to address.

Having an Outward View is a very critical component of the values that a Venture should cultivate. I would strongly advise a conscious plan and effort for this, with documentation, dissection, absorption and assimilation into your own 'go to market' journey. Its upsides are astronomical and its downsides are devastating. Take your pick!!

Chapter 7

HANDCUFFS & SHACKLES

Handicaps as challenges, the Credibility Gap, product and service offering perception, price and value connotations, Supplier and Partner skepticism, Process lacunae, People and Quality challenges, Market Intelligence handicap, The Financial Squeeze.

"Our performance on all counts sucks! We are sub-par on our delivery, service and product! What is happening?" Jay, the CEO of SmartKitchen Aids, uttered in frustration.

"Customer feedback is abysmal, complaints are rampant, and I do not see a word of appreciation in all that I have personally reviewed." Jay continued.

The Executive Review meeting for the month was on, and most of his 15 employees were in the room.

"We are not getting the best material and production standards from our partners. Our cost structures don't permit us to push for higher quality products," said his Chief Operating Officer and Co-promoter, Ulhas.

"There have also been delays in supplies and installation support. Customers and Distributors are getting frustrated with our product and service." This from the Sales Manager, Sunil, who bore the brunt of their angst.

"They are capitalizing on this opportunity. The payments for the supplies are being deliberately delayed by them, using this as an excuse," was the sage observation from the Finance head, Parthasarathy, a young, recent hire. "Our cash flows and cash position are a matter of grave concern."

"Who is following up for the payments? Didn't we all agree to keep our eye on it as priority?" Jay questioned.

Salaries have got delayed as a consequence and morale is down", Shruti, the HR manager, piped in.

"It is becoming progressively difficult to hold on to the people we have, and hiring is a challenge too, as they do not speak well of us to the potential candidates." She continued, looking really worried.

Jay and Ulhas, the two Founders, looked at each other, and their shoulders dropped, with the realization dawning on them, that the problem was multidimensional, with no easy solution. It was not going to get resolved in this meeting, and called for a longer, serious think.

I am sure a number of Founders of Start-ups can relate to this completely. One of the realities of venturing on one's own, is the dilemma of dealing with the various handicaps and challenges that bombard you in the first few months. Cliched as it may sound, the fact remains that the smaller you are, the greater these hurdles to surmount.

As business progresses, these will gradually taper off and there is a certain size one needs to achieve before some breathing space can be created; albeit with caveats, which we shall talk about later.

It's important to understand and absorb the following realities, as acceptance is half the battle won.

1. **Handicaps are here to stay.** Accept this first, as that will make you think of ways of dealing with it, get into the solution mode, and away from the problem. Acceptance of an issue, is a major step and half the battle. All aspects of the business will throw up these, in various forms

and manner. Learn to deal with it! Your venture is an unknown entity, possibly claiming to be a disruptor, promising quality and excellence across the board, with a team which is still wet under the ears! Under these circumstances, there is bound to be a certain scepticism amongst all involved parties and entities, be it customers, suppliers, partners and employees. These will translate into quality issues, supply defaults, product failures, poor trust, and payment stress. Each of these constituents will translate their scepticism into lowering their own standards, commitments, focus and diligence, for your offering, in everything they do. These will be the handicaps that you need to deal with. Staying in a denial mode will only increase the size of the problem, by the time you come to realise, accept, and get around to addressing it. Please acknowledge this fact, and you will be better able to negotiate this pitfall.

2. **The Credibility Gap.** The first and foremost issue which will confound you will be the fact that every interaction you have, will throw up a number of objections, doubts, questions, all emerging from the fact that there is zero credibility, for what you say or promise, to begin with. The perception will be one of a 'One day

wonder', here today, gone tomorrow, and this will show up in every interaction, negotiation, documentation or dealing that you do. You in turn, will keep wondering why is it that they are treating our venture differently? Aren't we also in the same market, operating on the same lines? The unpalatable truth of this behaviour trait, is the resolute lack of basic trust, faith and credibility. No one will voice it, but it will be the tenet on which they will all deal with you. Being sensitive to this, and managing your communication and dealings with this firmly in the background, is the only way forward. My suggestion has always been, and will be, under-promise and deliver, if not over-deliver. Do not make any statement or commitment you cannot demonstrate and ratify by your actions, very clearly, else you have lost the battle here itself. Let your actions and performance work its way, to undermine this rather unilateral and unfair negative bias. The various shapes and sizes in which these rear their head, we shall now talk about.

3. **Product and Service Offering Perception.** This is probably the biggest handicap and negative bias that you will be confronted with. It will start with your own people, in most cases. Show

them the product, and a comparison with what is available, but there will be scant acceptance of the data and information, to begin with. There will be a question mark on quality, price, longevity, delivery, installation and servicing, maybe the data presented too, even from your own people. Accept this as a fact, and do not end up fighting it, as else you would have lost the internal ambassadors. Often, it makes sense to allow the employees to try it, get a feel for it, keep a working model in the office, use it yourself as the promoter, to demonstrate and ratify your own confidence in it. Take their feedback and suggestions and share your willingness to, showing you have an open mind. The partners and dealers will have even more concerns and doubts. In a B to B situation, it prompts questions on the longevity of the company itself, and hence non acceptance of the product or service. The background of Founders, their industry experience, the names associated with the business as Advisors, the Shareholders and Investors, will all come under scrutiny, as a surrogate to evaluate the probability and likelihood of the Venture surviving for a reasonable period of time. There are no shortcuts and easy answers to deal with this. Communicate honestly and sincerely your own confidence and faith, your belief and openness, for it to rub off on the other constituents. This exercise is something that does have a long life-cycle, and calls for constant reiteration.

4. **Price and Value Connotations.** More often than not, such perceptions remain unstated, and reflect in the way the customer, partner, dealer or intermediary evaluates the price point of your offering, and the other terms. A better product or service, feature for feature with the key competitor, will still need to be discounted vis-à-vis the established product or service, thanks to this liability or handicap. It gets compounded by the fact that the first few customers, the early risk takers, who take the first plunge with anything new, are typically more astute, demanding, hard negotiators, knowledgeable and savvy, and are aware they can, and will extract their pound of flesh. Be it price, credit terms, service standards, freebies, bundling or anything else they can think of! Be aware of this, and steel yourself for a long-drawn battle for it. If you give in too easy, they will perceive it as your own lack of confidence in your offering. It will mean long business development cycles to begin with, and

you need to grit your teeth and stay the course. There are no workarounds to this; make sure the transaction translates into a gain in perception, at every interaction with such customers. In most cases, if you do not give in easily, it has a very positive rub-off, and normally ends with grudging respect, as long as the process remains pleasant and transparent.

5. **Supplier & Partner Scepticism.** In the early days, one other fallout of the credibility conundrum is the lack of confidence that suppliers and partners have in you and the Organization. It will reflect in everything; the time and attention you get from them, their payment terms and pricing, their people and responses to your queries and demands, their willingness to extend themselves for you, their payments and billing, their ability to accommodate peaks and troughs in demands, as well as their openness to new ideas and suggestions. You have to bite the bullet, stay the course and slowly create the necessary comfort and confidence, for this scepticism to die its natural death. Any visible aggressive effort to challenge or call out this behaviour may only result in them shutting you out, and terminating the relationship, prematurely. It can be very

demoralizing and will probably affect the morale of your team, and you as promoters, as well. It's a thin line you have to walk, swallowing pride and ego, and accept the reality as a genuine challenge.

6. **Process Lacunae.** It's a given that the first few attempts at following a process for supply and execution of the product or service, are bound to throw up huge unanticipated pitfalls, shortcomings and gaps in the process. Often the result of rudimentary early-stage awareness and anticipation, your people will also tend to throw in the towel, at the earliest sign of non-conformation, or rethink. Hence, the need to pilot, monitor and track every stage of the process for inputs, processing quality and outputs, and retool and modify the steps if need be, is a must. There are no shortcuts to this; there is often sage advice about getting it right the first time; well said, but tends to fail in totally new organizations and their processes. Time and resources starved, most times the Start-ups have to alter on-the-fly, tweak the steps, get closer to the desired quality and time benchmark, they had set for themselves. It may take a few iterations, but easier to do, when there are only a few transactions and exchanges with

customers. Personal involvement and interaction can help minimise the downside of such failures or shortcomings. Stay on top of it, and in close quarters to begin with.

7. **People & Quality Challenges.** The largest and most underrated challenge is the challenge of getting good quality people and the best performance and output from them. The truth of the matter is that in the early stages, with poor credibility and awareness, you do not always have the choice of the best resources, eager to be part of your Venture. If you find some, you need to get rid of your confirmation bias, and check as to why someone of the sterling profile, would deign to be part of a Start-up like yours. This healthy cynicism often is a prudent one to prevent hiring mistakes; an error driven by the naïve flattering belief that you are being seen as a sought-after employer, can be extremely damaging, and have very serious consequences in the early stage. An Organization of close friends, went through an unfortunate experience of making this error, and paid a huge price in terms of time, cost and morale of the set up.

The reality is that most of your hires in the early stages will have to be a 'will do' standard, not the best in class and desired standard. Your Ventures' credibility and awareness, the ability to compensate, the promise of a future career, growth and role expansion are all up in the air, and neither can you promise or guarantee these. This handicap is always an issue, and needs to be understood and factored into all decisioning. There are and will be exceptions; but do not plan for them. Your onus should be on meeting the minimum standard that you have set for the Venture. People grow as Organizations grow! All this will mean that output and deliverables from the team, will also be only of a certain level. I often advise pragmatism and acceptance of average or barely above average performance under the circumstances; It will require extensive handholding, monitoring and course correcting to get them to get up the quality curve. Accept this as a reality!

8. **Gaps in Market Intelligence.** In the early days, you will often find that competitors have made moves and changes, which you are blissfully unaware of. Its par for the course. Don't beat yourself or your team up for it! Your intelligence gathering mechanism is also handicapped, because of all the above, and often you will be the last to know of even monumental changes in the market place. Errors of

judgement, pricing, service, partner appointments and terms, employees hiring and their decisions, are all fall outs of this truth. Take these in your stride. A good way would be to mentally prepare yourself and anticipate it. Anything else, unfortunately, will be wishful thinking on your part. You and your Co-Founders need to be grounded enough to swallow disappointment and setbacks, and look ahead all the time. Mistakes are part and parcel of the journey; beating oneself up or employees up, does nothing but impact your own motivation, and team morale adversely!

9. **The Financial Squeeze.** The biggest elephant in the room, possibly for most start-ups. It's a hand-to-mouth journey, in the bootstrapping days, and often will mean zero cash balances or bank balances, even with revenues coming in. Plan for this eventuality, and pray it does not happen! Unforeseen circumstances like the pandemic apart, there are innumerable assumptions on cash flow that go wrong, often the result of one or more of the factors listed above. The Finance Manager will have his hands full; that individual will need to be someone who is of a very strong constitution and well versed with the nuances of managing finances of this nature. The default

option suggested by me always to Founders, is to do it yourself with a Chartered Accountant's help, till such time you have a capital infusion and can breathe easy with a clear window of at least 18 months, to hire someone senior for this. May sound a bit harsh, but better safe than sorry, I guess. My advice would also be to keep a very close tab on the outflows especially, and track cash positions almost with a religious fervour! It pays off handsomely in the long run.

The crunch can also impact basic pay-outs; salaries, statutory payments, taxes are often the first to get the axe. Nothing can be farther from the truth. Make sure these remain your top three priorities for the venture, as they have serious long-term ramifications, and tend to rear their heads, at most inopportune times. The discretionary expenses, and that includes your own spends as Founders, and your own take-home compensation, should be your focus. A close tab on the cash position will also ensure you begin to think of the effort to raise money. It may mean it may have to be an exercise you undertake a little earlier than planned, which you will be able to see and anticipate, if you are tracking and monitoring cash flows and budgets.

These, as a bunch of handicaps are in no way a full list; there would be others specific to the industry, the business, the country, the geography, the local variations and preferences, the local laws and taxes, and so on. However, an appreciation of the terrain of the journey on which you have embarked, and better anticipation of challenges and pitfalls, will ensure you have thought through your strategies to deal with them a little in advance, and they don't catch you napping, when they do hit you!!

Chapter 8

THE FUND-RAISING JOURNEY

Approach with caution, there are no free lunches, seek like-minded Investors, It's a journey, not the end, Stay Pragmatic and Honest, Promise only what is likely to be achieved, Carry your Co-Founders along, Appreciate the long term implications, Understand the small print, Seek guidance from mentors, find Financial expertise to enable the transaction, Documentation and Legal Paperwork is critical.

"Sir, we have been shortlisted by six Angel and Venture groups, for possible funding" Anand's voice over the phone was bursting with excitement, as he started his fortnightly session with me.

"That's good. Hope at least one of them translates into a Term Sheet for you. Tell me more about this and how it transpired." I responded in a cautious manner.

My response to his excited utterance, I could sense, did deflate him a bit.

"We had a fast-dating kind of pitching session, organised by a local facilitator, and we pitched to 8 of them, five minutes each Venture, and six of them have shown prima facie interest," Anand was back to his exuberant self.

"The Organizer felt that we were possibly the best in terms of our pitch and focus, and the value proposition. Thank you for your guidance and help in sharpening our pitch and making us good at it."

He was referring to the new pitch document and presentation rehearsals which I had put them through earlier, to get them up the curve on how to talk to potential investors.

"I would advise against getting distracted from the business till we see something concrete from at least one of them. You have been through this, and by now should be wise enough." Was my caution for him.

"The business and its growth should continue to be priority number one" I added, to reinforce the point.

"Sir, this time was different. Because of Covid, all presentations were on Zoom, and brief and focussed.

They responded immediately with good questions and showed high interest." Anand was getting excited once again.

"They did not have a choice, and all of them are forced to go this route. They are getting used to this approach. How many Ventures were pitching to them?" my questioning continued.

"There were 12 Start-ups who pitched, and we were one of those who got favourable responses, according to the Organizers. Hence, I am very hopeful," Anand responded.

"Let's see how things pan out. Meanwhile, get back to focussing on the growth journey, Anand. Don't let yourself get distracted. You remember what happened the last time you were approached by a plethora of investors and you chased them to no avail. You did compromise on the growth and thus delayed the revenue commencement in the previous year. How many did you interact with? About 20 if I am not wrong?"

My gentle reminder of the previous experiments into raising capital, got him thinking.

"You are right Sir. Will not make the same mistake again." He said, after a brief pause.

"Don't discount the pitching that you did. You did well. Wait for a concrete response before you get your hopes up," to ensure he did not lose his morale or lose confidence in the process.

All Start-ups, at some point in their early journey, do wake up to the need for raising capital. While debt can be an option too, and will throw some light on that later, the cycle of capital raising can be very educational, taxing, stressful, full of surprises and setbacks, sobering, and by and large something that you are neither prepared for, or fully aware and appreciative of.

It is indeed a venturing into a realm of the unknown, for most founders and promoters, and the need for a mentor, guide and hand-holder cannot be more emphasized. Investment bankers fill this role partly, but unfortunately their approach and focus remain largely transaction oriented, and thus at times fail to provide the complete perspective and guidance that the Promoters and their Ventures need.

The challenges and pitfalls of this journey are many and multi-faceted; add to that the fact that this is your first serious exposure to this world of Venture and Seed funds, Private Equity Funds, Strategic Individual Investors and Angel networks.

Some pointers to the approach and thinking to guide you, I would like to suggest at this juncture.

1. **Approach with Caution.** As you get pulled into this process of seeking investors and fund raising, the first thing you need is a healthy dose of scepticism and caution. The scepticism should be in terms of the expectation of results and success, the time lines for this exercise, the rock star image of the Company the interest and commitment signs and messages, and the end-of-the-road visibility. It is never as easy, short or simple as we assume. Stories and tales of how easily or quickly successful venture did it, tend to colour and distort the picture. Yes, there are success stories of first attempt lucky hits, but they are exactly that. Don't get into the survivors' bias, and assume just because you see one, all venture have similar stories. The fund-raising exercise is a challenge in itself, and can often extend to a year or more! Make sure it doesn't distract and fully overwhelm you into losing your oversight on your business in the bargain. Be cautious about ensuring you don't lose focus on your ultimate objective and goal, to make the venture a growing and successful one!

2. **There are no Free Lunches.** An unpalatable truth of this process, that most promoters fail to see, remains the fact that any capital raise, at every stage of the journey, comes with its caveats. There are genuinely no free lunches. If anything, the sacrifices sometimes appear larger than the gains made. The Capital helps scale the business but the quid pro quo is not something that can be either wished away or conveniently ignored. My advice to Founders would be simply this: be conscious of this phenomenon, and please critically understand and evaluate what you are giving up for it. It could be Board seats, and hence accountability to outsiders, executive decisioning by way of strictures, rights and entitlements, flexibility on strategy, long term vision compromises, parts of culture and values, partnerships and alliances because of investor affiliations, additional costs for mandated new hires, and so on. While it is logical for any investor to seek certain privileges for enabling and supporting your growth as a Venture, do keep in mind that at times, there would be potential conflicts which could raise their head, if not immediately, down the line for sure. Please spend time doing 'worst case' scenario building

to visualize and appreciate the downsides of the caveats and their implications.

3. **Seek Like-Minded Investors.** It becomes extremely important to thus ensure, that there is at least a meeting of minds in most areas of philosophy, vision, beliefs and values, with the potential investor or investing companies. Kindly do adequate research, and get some intelligence on the Investor, from all angles. Your knowledge of market intelligence should come in handy in going about this exercise, and your mentor, who is likely to be a seasoned professional, can add value to it. A quality due diligence of potential Investors and Investor Companies, is always a good practice even before you receive and seriously consider their Term Sheet. It is not mandatory to accept the first one that is presented to you, even though the pressures on the cash position and finances may dictate otherwise. Do not jump at the first potential partner that surfaces, and accept their Term Sheet, before doing your own thorough due diligence. Better be safe than sorry!!

4. **It's a Journey, not the End.** Critical to remember this; the process of capital raising is not going to end with this round of funding. You will go on to further rounds; realize that the industry has gone

down the alphabet list for series of fund raisings, as a nomenclature! At every stage in this journey, there will invariably be an evaluation of who your current investors are, by the latest suitors; opportunistic decisions in the early stages, can isolate you from much better and valuable future entrants. I have had Founders of ventures meet me and regret some of their earlier compromises, which had helped them deal with the immediate crisis, but created insurmountable handicaps for times to come! The compromises are not easy to negate or get out of. Keep a long-term perspective while taking a short-term decision, in terms of who you choose as your financial partner in this long journey. Shy away from dubious, poor antecedents bearing, suspicious Organizations, offshore entities from unfriendly blacklisted nations, unknown sources of capital entities, as all of these can lead to serious repercussions of Compliance, and Regulatory retaliation and strictures. The path to success is littered with many such Ventures who got burnt due to their ignorance, greed or short sightedness.

5. **Stay Pragmatic & Honest.** During this entire process of wooing and being wooed, by Funders and Investors, stay true to your own reality, your

deliverable plans, your beliefs and commitments, and your long-term objectives. The temptation to tweak your pitch, to make it very attractive for the Investors, and get you a better valuation, is often the credo and practice in the Industry. Making an impactful pitch, with data presented to create an attractive proposition, is a given and should be done! But, do not tweak and inflate your data on projections, and profitability to make the picture rosier! Investment Bankers will do what you desire and agree to, and hence their own perspective is limited in this regard, most times. My two-bits to you as Founders and Promoters would be to present yourself for what you are and likely to be. The stories and tall tales all come back to bite you in places which you do not like. This is my personal experience with a large number of them, who have gone down that path. It sets you up for a lose-lose, and no one really wins in this situation. Irrespective of who else is doing it, it still is a ticket for disastrous outcomes for a lifetime.

6. **Promise only what you are Convinced you can Deliver.** A controversial statement, as some would say you do not know what will happen in this journey, and cannot predict the future. True, but the wisdom lies in being realistic about the

projections of the future, and creating milestones and deliverables for yourself on that basis. It may translate into a lower valuation or a larger share for the Investor at this stage, but the future rounds become far more attractive in the process! By meeting, and exceeding if possible, your milestones deliverables in the defined timeframes, you position yourself way up the curve for your next round of fund raising and associated valuations. Many a promoter group, has ended up shooting themselves in the foot, by overcommitting, and in the process failing to deliver. This has created bad blood, loss of control, share devaluation, lower stake for promoters, and in some cases, even long drawn litigation and stress. Please ask yourself if you are willing to live with the consequences of letting greed and avarice drive you.

7. **Carry your Co-founders Along.** May sound very basic, but you would be surprised at the number of cases where this has led to the downfall of the Venture itself. When the process of fund raising starts, individual ambitions, risk taking ability, expectations, influences and drivers will vary across the founding team. I have often been witness to long drawn battles, feelings of mistrust, open feuds, turf wars, and physical hurts and threats,

which is a sure-shot journey to destruction. Even before the journey begins, you must have a shared approach to the fund raise, establish principles and guidelines for decisioning, agree on information sharing and update pacts, identify a point person for the process, minimum valuation and desired valuation numbers, a walk away number, a non-negotiable and deal breaker terms list, we could go on. The sum and substance of this is: do some serious preparatory work, before you embark on this part of the journey of Fund Raising. Get on the same page, and do it together. Many a venture which failed to do this has had to do this, has had to settle for short changed and compromised deals, with creation of long-lasting animosity and bitterness, in the process. A well thought out and executed fund raising exercise is a sure preventive. That will probably result in the entire effort ending in a win-win for all!!

8. **Fully Appreciate the Long-Term Implications.** The euphoria of a Term Sheet cannot be understated; calls for celebration and rightfully so. Please do not let this blind you to the implications of who you sign up with, what you sign up for, and how much you are giving up. Most Term Sheets, apart from the amount being offered and equity

sought for it, come with a number of other clauses, which always have long term ramifications. Please spend some time to understand these clauses and their implications. Use sounding boards, experts & professionals, and mentors & advisors to dwell on them, discuss them threadbare, build scenarios around them, and then figure out if you can live with the worst-case fallout of these. It's called going in with eyes open. In the scenarios you build, do think of growth and future, environment changes, 'Black Swan' happenings like Covid, Compliance and Regulatory framework changes, global impactful upheavals, and disruptive new offerings and Ventures as well. Can you live with the implications of these clauses in all these scenarios?? If yes, please go ahead with gusto!!

9. **Read the Fine Print.** The translation of the Term Sheet into a Share Holders and Share Purchase Agreement, invariably brings in new clauses, additional protective covenants and more, as the lawyers get to work on it. It makes immense sense to whet every clause of the Agreement, understand and appreciate the ramifications. Do not make the mistake of not reading and understanding every clause you sign up for. Appreciate that the Investor or Investing Company, have spent years

to build, acquire and hone the skills at precisely that. Hence, every word of what they ask you to sign up for, should and will be keeping their interest and benefits in mind. They are and will be completely professional and even hard-nosed about it, and in some cases may even be a 'no holds barred' approach as well. It is in your Venture's and your own interest to dissect everything you are potentially signing, and understanding every interpretation of what it portends. Abundant caution and due diligence with an eye for detail, can and will stand you in very good stead in this journey you have begun.

10. **Lean on your Mentor.** Please make it a point to involve your mentor, and pick their brains on the process and discussions, and get his or her perspectives on the document you are about to sign. They, in their own journeys, would have seen and dealt with such situations aplenty. Goes without saying, that this experience of theirs, and stature and maturity, is more likely to result in sage, pragmatic wisdom from them. Leverage this to your advantage. None of us come fully loaded into the world of business with complete understanding of the nuances and vagaries of the trade and ecosystem. These are best appreciated

and garnered from people who have seen and done that before. There is no ignominy in accepting your own handicap in this area, and putting yourself in front of them, seeking hand-holding and guidance, to avoid the pitfalls of this process.

11. **Seek Financial Expertise.** Worth reiterating a number of times, please involve your Chartered Accountant and financial expert in this challenging journey of raising capital. It is something that you cannot do without, and please do not cut corners on this, and let cost considerations drive your thoughts. You will short change yourself. There are critical junctures in the business growth cycle, where a compromise can damage the Venture for a lifetime. When raising capital, see the cost of a Financial Expert an as investment especially when you are seeking one, and err on the side of caution. A qualified and competent Chartered Accountant can be the difference between a sub optimal and poor deal going through, or you pulling off a really good beneficial deal, for you as Founders, and the Organization.

12. **Documentation and Legal Paperwork are Paramount.** I have been a witness to too many

situations where poor quality of documentation and paperwork, have resulted in promoters losing critical legal battles, and sometimes, control of their company, in the process. When they were going through the documentation, their focus was on getting the money in the bank as quickly as possible, given their dire situation on finances, and hence ended up glossing over potentially explosive clauses and their implications. The business journey ahead, will have its ups and downs, and every clause has to be looked at from the worst-case scenario, understood with its implications fully, and only then accepted. Get good legal help to ensure this, but there is none better than you yourself to think through them, as you appreciate the business nuances that will be at work in times to come. Make sure you and your co-founders personally have spent adequate time and digested each clause and its implication. Take your time, consult experts and advisors, digest it fully, before you give a go ahead and accept each clause of the agreement and ratify the final document. Don't make haste in the anxiety to get the funds in, and lock yourself in, into a lose-lose situation.

This is possibly the first inflexion point of the journey, and the complexities of building and growing the Venture increase substantially with the addition of an investor or investors is of paramount importance that you start this stage of the journey with the right moves, and on firm footing. As Founders, abundant caution and diligence the first time you do this, adds tremendously to your ability and propensity to attract and raise subsequent rounds of capital. Go right ahead, and get this done, once you have run through this gamut of pointers. Your ability to negotiate and navigate through the challenges and pitfalls of fund raising will be significantly enhanced post that, and improve the probability of a great start in that direction.

Chapter 9

PEOPLE & TEAM BUILDING

Look for enthusiasm and attitude, Hire fit-for-purpose, Open and Honest communication, Celebrate small wins, Engage beyond work, Share vision and objectives often, Recognize, Reward and share spoils, Hire to grow, Clarify Roles and Responsibilities frequently, Set benchmarks for Standards of performance, Lead by example, Use performance based compensation, Keep the Organization Lean, Integrity & Sharing Norms.

A dejected bunch of three morose faces, confronted me, as I walked into the coffee shop, for the monthly chat with the Co-Founders of the Fintech start up.

"Why the glum looks? The world is not coming to an end." I opened, trying to lighten the mood.

Roopa, the CEO of the venture, opened up "We have lost 3 people in the last 30 days and are back to square one. How do we build a business if we keep losing people?"

"One of them was a Senior Executive we had got in at a very high compensation, and after making major compromises" Sandeep, her partner and COO chipped in. "He walked away after 4 months and we could do nothing." He continued.

"We took a serious hit on our cash flows and cash positions to get him in. It also created repercussions in terms of the rest of the team. Our credibility with clients and partners has also been dented in the process." Sunil, the CFO and third partner in the venture, voiced.

"Forget that. He anyway created more trouble for us with the team, when he was there." Roopa started justifying the exit, and rationalizing to herself.

"The other two were actually better performers, but had aspirations and expectations which we could not fulfil. It resulted in slippages in their performance too." Sandeep continued, looking terribly dejected.

"It has pushed us back by at least six months now, in our journey. Our milestones for the first year, will now have to be seriously scaled down. Our runway for cash breakeven is now even longer, thanks to our big push for senior executives, while our cash reserves are depleted, and we are likely to feel the crunch within 3 months." Sunil, the numbers focussed finance expert opined.

"Where are we going wrong? We even gave all of them a very relaxed and easy work schedule, while we were pulling hard on all fronts. We wanted them to settle down, and not get scared away by the work pressure."

"We do admit that the atmosphere in the office has been a little strained and down, as all three of us, have been swamped and are struggling to get things going. It has impacted our own behaviour too."

Roopa, honestly voiced what I was sure all of them were thinking and feeling.

"Can you please help us think through this, and figure out how to go about it better?" Sandeep asked, looking at me expectantly, hoping I would give them some pointers.

I spent the next 60 minutes walking them through some critical pointers and suggestions, on creating, hiring, and building teams and Organizations. A very critical component of building a successful enterprise, that often tends to become the bugbear of budding ventures. Unfortunately, the criticality of this hits us only when we are chin deep and drowning. This is one of the largest challenges, that will confront you as Entrepreneurs, and the pitfalls in this are many. If we keep some of these pointers in mind, it helps us navigate this difficult minefield without serious damage to the Venture, Business and People, including the Promoters. Manage these well, and you are likely to come out on top with a cohesive, motivated, humming and driven team and Organization.

1. **Look for Enthusiasm and Attitude.** While hiring the first few people, please use this as the first filter for selection. In the early days, the structures, processes, standards, awareness, knowledge are still nascent, and in the formative stage. It often translates into chaos and bedlam in the office and the venture. Such times, there should be a premium on positivity, enthusiasm, willingness to learn, going beyond the brief or role, as that will make the difference between the new members deserting ship within months, or working with you as Founders to strengthen the foundation of the venture. May sound very cliched, but there is a lot of truth in this. Not everyone can function in a disorganised, unstructured, chaotic environment. I have often found this a handicap in most hires from very large, formally structured organizations who make the jump to a start-up, lured by the glamour and excitement of one! Not having been exposed

to an unstructured and chaotic environment, the propensity to feel lost and disoriented is very high. Being an early-stage venture, there is also very little by way of induction and direction that you end up providing, and this can leave individuals with low enthusiasm and initiative, at a loss! While exceptions do exist, the early indicator is their attitude and positivity. Please evaluate for these more critically, as knowledge and skills can be imparted with training and hand holding, but attitude is a long and often rare, improvement cycle!

2. **Hire Fit for Purpose.** I have often found early-stage Companies, going big bang, and hiring stalwarts from the related industry, like Roopa had done. A senior banker, the Managing Director of one of the verticals of the banks business running into billions, was a very exciting prospect, and a big feather their cap! A long, hard-negotiated deal was struck, where the compensation had to be in line with the seniority, experience and at par with last role, and reputation of the Organization. The result was it created a deep impact on the cash position and cash flow, with over 30% of the total Employee cost, being the cost of this one individual. High fixed compensation to attract,

notice period to pay off, were needed to close, and was complied with.

A very critical error in hiring, which a number of early-stage enterprises make. The opportunity to make a big hire as a coup, is often too good to ignore, and promoters succumb to the temptation of taking that risk. My advice to my mentees has always been, 'Hire Fit for Purpose.' Do not hire a General where a Lieutenant will do. Else you are failing everyone involved: yourself, your Venture and the individual you are hiring. If the role today, or in the next 18 months does not justify the seniority and experience, give it a pass, irrespective of how attractive and tempting the opportunity may be! It can easily become a white elephant for you, creating long lasting damage, with no upsides. You are the best judge of this, and please use your own counsel to take the call. I have often come across Promoter CEOs who have regretted succumbing to external pressures and opinions, from friends, influencers, partners, investors and forgetting that the buck stops with them. You, as Founders, will have to live with the decision and the individual, for better or for worse.

3. **Open & Honest Communication.** Begin with the hiring interviews itself. Refreshing honesty and openness always works in creating in people the right impression, that they can trust you. I have seen the opposite behaviour as the norm: the job, the Venture, the compensation, the infrastructure, are all glamorised and 'sold' to the potential candidates. It is a very short-term, transactional view, and takes away from the longevity and sustainability of the decision and the hire. The early hires are the ones you want should stay, be passionate like you, contribute and grow both themselves and the Enterprise, working shoulder to shoulder with you, as part of the founding team. Please let them know the lay of the land as is, but do share your own vision and plans of where you want to take the venture to. Trust is paramount in Organization building, and honesty and transparency in every communication, is a non-negotiable to help create a culture of true value and integrity.

It applies equally to good and bad news, and you need to develop the maturity and balance to be able to communicate both, with equal honesty. Do not get carried away, or swayed by either their seniority, experience, age, education qualifications, or previous designations. You cannot let that limit you from open discussions, feedback or even communicating a parting of ways with wrong hires! Roopa and her team, lived with it for a few extra months, losing a lot in the bargain, due to their reluctance to cut their losses and call a spade a spade!

Day to day communications too, need this as a philosophy. In the early stages, you do not have the luxury of making too many errors, or carrying passengers in your team. Hence being a little forthright, and communicating your vulnerability as an Enterprise to absorb the implications of such actions upfront and quickly, is a given! The lack of ability to carry and provide for such errors in judgement, is a handicap that you carry as the Start-up, invariably in the early days. Over time, as the venture grows, it will become progressively easier, as scale and better cash reserves, revenues, profits and investment capital, will give you some laxity and leeway to indulge.

4. **Celebrate Small Wins.** Motivating the team, and in the process yourself too, calls for a conscious effort to celebrate small wins. In the early stages, they are not very frequent, or of substance, very often. It is however, critical to do this, as it works

as an up-lifter of morale, and a good glue to bind the team together. Fellowship is the benefit that emerges, and goes a long way in building a cohesive driven Organization. These need not necessarily be grand celebrations or a night out for the team. Even sharing pizzas or samosas, and the office coffee, works in such cases! Make them impromptu, and in-the-moment occasions, and you will be surprised with the participation and the mood upliftment it can generate. Don't miss such opportunities ever, and you will see a far more resilient, unified, committed and passionate team at work! Make the workplace a place of warmth, passion, joy and camaraderie, as you put together your Venture, from the very beginning. As time moves on, this will translate into a culture and philosophy of the Enterprise, and will add to the edge that you will create as a positive, enthusiastic, charged and driven Organization.

5. **Engage beyond Work.** One of the underlying behaviours of good teams, is this overlap of their engagement beyond work environment and occasions. Make the time and create opportunities to engage beyond office and work-related issues. Movies, art, drama, bowling, social service are all ways and means of doing so. It creates a more

meaningful engagement for the employees and builds a stronger affinity with the Venture, and you, as a leader or leaders. I have often witnessed Start-up Founders not knowing anything about their employees beyond their role and responsibilities. One way of getting to know your team members, and for them to get to know you better, is to create such opportunities of engaging beyond work and work-related activities. Even impulsive Friday get-togethers with activities and games, and music and fun, should be good to begin with. However, please ensure you do get genuinely involved in these. As a leader and Founder, do make time to enthusiastically participate and be one of them; any pretences at being concerned and interested in your employees, are easy to sense, especially when the team is very small. We often tend to underestimate their ability to read this, to our detriment. Don't go down that path!!

6. **Share Vision and Objectives Often.** Teams perform best when they work with a purpose towards a common goal. As leaders, the Founders are primarily responsible for creating a purpose, by defining a vision and translating this into short and medium-term objectives. Please find the time and place as promoters for you to arrive

at the vision for the Venture early, as it will make this task easier when employees join you. In the journey of creating a successful business, there will be moments where you will feel the need, or circumstances will necessitate a revision and change, in the vision and long-term objectives. Revisit, rethink and reformulate it as many times as you think it is necessary, but do have one which is known to, and understood clearly by all. The key here is communication. Team and Organization building rests on the bedrock of communication; in the early days, it is even more so. There is nothing called over-communicating. Do not miss any opportunity to share, reiterate and remind every employee of what the Venture stands for, the problem and customer need it is addressing, and the Vision it is working towards. It need not be limited to verbal communication. Mails, WhatsApp messages, posters, laptop wallpapers are all fair game!! You will need to lead this from the front. Your own passion and commitment to it, will only further cement the team's determination and focus in making that happen!

7. **Recognize, Reward and Share Spoils.** While this is a tenet for most successful and well-oiled Organizations, as Start-ups you need to start this

process early, to keep the tempo, enthusiasm and morale up, through the tricky early years, more than ever! As human beings, one of our core needs is appreciation and recognition for a job well done, and it is largely independent of anything else that you may do for the team. Public appreciation, small rewards and prizes, memorabilia and visible aids for prominence, all go miles in this process. Nothing is too small or insignificant in the early days. Sharing the spoils, is a nuanced and different initiative. Do make sure to share the benefits of large deals, customer acquisitions, costs savings and anything else which contributes to the bottom line of the Venture, as well. The frequency and size of these, will perforce be at longer time intervals, and higher monetary values. Critical that you get the message across that you believe in genuinely sharing, and not just in tokens of appreciation. It will help you, at a later stage, to keep employees committed to you and the Venture. There will be periods of struggle, tough times and fierce competition, unforeseen challenges, and the confidence and commitment built in the early days, through such thoughtful gestures, will stand you in good stead.

8. **Hire to Grow.** In the hiring process, while you should not hire the most experienced, senior hires you can find, (Remember fit for purpose.), as a rule, it is however prudent to look for individuals who demonstrate the maturity and attitude to grow with the venture, into more complex and higher roles. In other words, the best employees are those who can grow as the Enterprise grows. This should be your core principle for hiring, as it is important you do not have to revisit every employee as your venture scales up, as you realize the Venture has outgrown them. In that eventuality, it will lead to a complete change of the team, and the continuity which is crucial for a cohesive and bonded team, will be lost. The values, culture, commitment, ethics and camaraderie will all need to be rebuilt and strengthened every time this happens, and will mean hard work to just keep the engine going!! At the same time, internal growth of a few employees into higher roles and positions, sends a very positive and encouraging message to the rest. Your ability to retain and control attrition also improves. Critical to remember, it's always easier to retain, than hire and train, both in terms of costs and efforts!

9. **Clarify Roles & Responsibilities.** In a rapidly growing Organization, the roles and responsibilities of team members undergoes rapid change too! As more people join in, the propensity to increase specialization and demarcation of roles for focus and delivery, is a given. You, as the Founders yourselves, will find you need to let go of a few things, delegate and review only, and move on, as the complexities and the nuances of the Venture start to explode. Under these circumstances, the employees will also see change happening, and it tends to create insecurities and concerns in their minds. A proactive process of redefining, communicating, documenting and reviewing against these, goes a long way in assuaging these feelings and fears. It is advisable that every month or few months, you sit down with each one, and reconfirm, recommunicate the role and its responsibilities and its deliverables as outputs from them. You need to use this opportunity to also review and share their own performance and recognise contribution or identify lacunae in their own deliverables. It also prepares them and gives them the focus to keep their own deliverables, role and responsibilities in the forefront of all they do on a daily basis. This should be on your checklist

and calendar, as a must do, to ensure you do not forget.

10. **Set Benchmarks for Performance Standards.** One challenge that Start-ups need to confront early, to ensure a smooth journey, is the setting of benchmarks and standards for every aspect of the business. Delivery times, price points, cost overruns, profitability, debtors' rates, timelines and bad debts, attrition rates, employee ratings, customer ratings, error rates, response times for service, service recovery timelines, quality standards, relative benchmarks with competition, are some of those that come to mind. Each one of these, then translates into deliverables for team members responsible for that aspect of the business. The fact is also, that these could be moving targets, which keep tightening or improving with time and changes in the environment, or strategy itself. It requires a strong will, determination and a healthy sense of self-worth to set these high, and work towards delivering on these standards. Build them up from a lower level, raising the bar at concrete intervals. The pitfall to avoid will be to set them too high, which makes it impossible to achieve, and results in everyone putting up their hands and letting things slide! These act as guidelines and

enable the team to stay focussed on the critical parameters, and ensure consistency, predictability, reliability and dependability become intrinsic to the Enterprise.

11. **Lead by Example.** One clear pitfall you as founders need to stay clear of; don't assume you are not under the purview of these benchmarks and standards, and can take a rain-check on performance. In the early stages, what is happening is visible to all, without filters or colours and twists to it. The scant proven credibility creates a very stringent and unforgiving environment for you as leaders. In a one-room office, it is apparent to one and all as to who is pulling their weight and who isn't. If anything, you need to dig in with far more fervour, to try and establish your own credentials as a hardworking team player. Hence, there is no option but to lead by example, in terms of efforts, standards, timelines, speed and flexibility in whatever you do. Simple things like office discipline, timings, breaks, consistency, transparency and equality are all out there for everyone to see and judge. It is also an irrefutable truth that any leeway you allow yourself, takes away your moral high ground to pull up anyone else for the same. Ground lost in this, unfortunately,

takes a long time for recovery as perception has a long tail, and lives for a long time. Even if with changing circumstances, people, and your own traits, have long undergone a change for the better, this is one faultline that does not easily go away!!

12. **Performance based Compensation.** Roopa's grave error in the incident earlier, was the fact that she forgot that in a Start-up Venture, compensation is always a combination of a lower fixed component, and performance-based incentives, variable pay and stock options too. While the candidates who you want to hire, may have notions of seeking a big jump, given they are jumping to an unknown risky proposition, you as the Founders and Promoters, cannot lose sight of your limitations and where you are! Over time, the risk that the candidate takes, in case he or she joins you, needs to be compensated for commensurately, but the components of that, should always be linked to their, and the Organization's performance. Honest communication of this philosophy while discussing and agreeing to this upfront, can save you and the company a lot of angst and heartburn in the years to come. The crux of the issue is this: there has to be some skin in the game for the candidates too; there are no free lunches for

anybody. It will result in a longer hiring cycle maybe, for some key positions, but it is worth the trouble. Someone who doesn't understand the rationality of this thinking and communication, may not be the most suitable candidate for a Venture like yours.

13. **Keep the Organization Lean.** As you build your team, the onus right through should be to keep the structure flat, till the complexities demand layering and specialised roles and responsibilities. The more layers you add, you tend to distance yourself from where the action is, and as a promoter, your eye on the ball is a given, for a long period of time. Don't fall for the temptation of making your own life simple, by creating a level of a senior management, with fancy designations in between, who you can then direct and review. It never works that way, in the early days. What happens is that information flow is the first thing that gets diluted and choked. You will start knowing less and less, and with significant delays, about what is actually happening. Hence, awareness of any crisis, which is a bugbear of a Start-up, will be delayed, diluted and distorted, by the time it reaches you. The cost of recovery and rectification, by then, would have grown

manifold, becoming more complex, with greater long-term consequences. Keep your hands dirty for as long as possible, at least till the Enterprise makes money and you have enough of it to absorb these shocks, and their resultant costs and setbacks.

14. **Integrity and Sharing Norms.** A separate mention of this is needed here. As you build a team and hire for the long term, you will be called upon to take a few tough decisions, in the interest of the Organization and Venture. The trade-offs will surface, such as integrity versus performance, loyalty versus delivery. Set your benchmark high and upfront on all of these. You should recognise integrity as a core value and keep a very high bar on it. In a crux, it would be prudent to let the person go, if he or she is of questionable integrity, irrespective of performance on the job. It sets the tone for the culture of the Organization, which is a long haul to build. Good to start early and clearly!

Loyalty and longevity are scarce commodities in the early stages of an Organization, and should rightfully be recognised and appreciated, along with performance. It is advisable to keep all stock options and other sharing measures largely back ended with long vesting periods, and linked to employee tenures and performance. It resonates well with the teams and also ensures there are no situations of employees exiting early, with vested shares to boot! Stocks need to be earned over a period of time, in line with Organization growth and prosperity, and by being a contributor to it.

Probably the most challenging task in building an Enterprise is the whole gamut of finding the right people, hiring them, motivating them, ensuring performance, justly evaluating and rewarding them, and in the process, binding them together as a team, for the long term. It remains the potential waterloo of most CEOs and promoters, and has often led to their ultimate downfall, and oblivion for the Venture itself! Tread with care and ensure you build on the opportunity to create history together.

Chapter 10

THE DEBT DELIBERATIONS

Not as easy as it seems, Sources and challenges, Costs and sacrifices, Bankers and their obsessions, The NBFC dilemma, Debt funds and Structured Debt, Trade-offs and implications, Payback and exits...

"We need to find some collateral, even from a third party if need be." Simon, the Co-Founder of the venture, voiced amidst the heated debate.

"Where do we go for it? The only option would be to ask our parents, which I am not willing to do." Arun responded, with resigned finality.

Arun and Simon had, with two other classmates, founded an Analytics Business. They were here today, to plan for the next steps in the journey, as they were now poised for the next phase of growth. This meeting was to iron out the nitty-gritties, and the source of funding for this growth.

They were, as usual, seated around the only table large enough in their office, to take all four of them- the two, with the other Co-Founders.

"The bankers won't budge on that requirement" Simon argued. As the CEO designate, apart from being the largest shareholder, he was keen that they closed out the fund requirements for the attractive, hard fought, long-term contract, that had finally materialized.

"May be true, but who do we ask? Is it a fair thing to seek your father's property as collateral? Are we ever going to pay back the bankers, and release the property we pledge?" Kushal, the third Co-Founder and the CFO designate, volunteered.

"Have also looked at another option from SmartBiz Finance. They are open to considering a smaller loan, but fully unsecured, as a business loan, which will however mean a larger monthly pay-out, as an equated monthly instalment, and needs to be fully paid back within three years," Kushal added.

"However, look at the cost. It is almost twice as expensive for us, apart from the fact that the loan size is meagre, and payback is a killer" said, Sundar, the last of the partners, and the COO of the team.

That put a brake on the discussion for a few seconds.

"What other options can we look at, Kushal?" Arun broke the silence.

"Are there other sources possible?" Simon, jumped in, taking charge of the discussion again.

"Have been approached by some Venture Debt Funds, but I am yet to study the structure, its cost and other implications" Kushal explained.

"Any of these will also take time and do we have the time before we can commence execution of the contract? Won't we miss some deadlines?" Sundar, intervened with his word of caution.

"The bankers are all set to go ahead, and we should have money in the bank, within a month, if we can provide the collateral worth 1.5 Crores. Their sanction letter, we have already received, and the only clause which is a show stopper is this." Simon elaborated.

"Once signed, the documentation can start and we will be well on the way towards money in the bank," he exclaimed, looking around the table.

"SmartBiz Finance has also given us the sanction letter, and there we can get the money in the bank in 2 weeks, if we are willing to live with the 60 Lacs they have approved." Kushal voiced, tabling the option available once again.

"Can't we manage with the 60 Lacs? We can keep looking meanwhile for the other debt fund options." Arun suggested.

"We don't want to go out again in 6 months' time for another loan, if we get our next contract. We do not have the luxury of keeping on raising debt." Simon defended.

"I can keep looking, and maybe get something going by then" Kushal hopefully added.

"Can you assure us that? What if we cannot? We would have lost the ability to get money in the bank worth 1.5 Crores." Simon retorted.

"It's not going to be money in the bank. It will be a line of credit which we can draw down upon" Kushal clarified.

"With the NBFC option, it is actually money in the bank" he further elaborated.

"Can we sleep over this, and maybe speak to someone, who can throw some light on this and its implications? I am not comfortable with this whole thought of asking Simon's father to put up his flat as collateral. Simon, very unfair to even ask him. He may not say no, but I am feeling guilty about it." Sundar, the voice of reason and pragmatism, voiced this in a measured manner, thus bringing the unfinished meeting to a close.

This reality confronts most start-ups as they start to ramp up their business, and the revenues start to pour in. It's a challenge which is real, but not something unwelcome. In most contracts, the fact remains that the costs are largely upfront, and the revenues are milestone based, and/or at deferred intervals. Moreover, the billing and payment cycle, even optimistically, in most cases, stretches to at least 90 days, if not more, thus leaving a gaping hole in the cash flows, which needs to be filled. It indeed was a problem that needed a solution before moving further with the contract.

The challenge here is not finding the funding, but understanding and absorbing the implications of the various options available, avoiding the pitfalls which, one not very knowledgeable, invariably fails to see. Some pointers, which may enable you to negotiate this minefield a little better, are presented below for you to mull over.

1. **Never as easy as it seems.** Raising debt, or borrowing for the business is seldom as simple as it is made out to be. The process itself is long, and there are myriad options to evaluate. The various aspects and nuances of each option, invariably

leads to spending hours, if not days deliberating and weighing the pros and cons of each option, and fully understanding the implications for the business. Good knowledge of finance is the basic requirement, and then come the whole series of data providing, due diligence, documentation, analysis, projections, personal records and information, credit evaluation, offer letters, agreements, regulatory filings and verifications, to name a few. All this requires diligence, an eye for detail, and patience and perseverance to negotiate, agree and close. A Finance Head, in most Start-ups may have the knowledge of some of these, but it invariably needs special experts and advisors to bridge the gaps. Do not begrudge and desist from seeking help to negotiate and successfully close this process. There may be costs associated with this, but see it as a worthwhile investment for the future of the business.

2. **Sources and Challenges.** The first major challenge, once you have made up your mind to go the debt route, after appropriate deliberations, is to identify the right source for the borrowings. Banks, Non-Banking Finance Companies, Quasi Government Financial Institutions, Debt Venture Funds, Individual lenders, Family Offices, Digital

Aggregators and facilitators, are all in play, at most times. The challenge does not end there. Each of these options have their own lending norms, quirks of busines practices, cost structures and pricing options, customised product offerings, timelines and compliance requirements, and documentation and review standards. Please evaluate and negotiate these with caution. Not only that, within each category, you will have multiple, competing players, with their own range of pricing, timelines, offerings, payback periods, documentation and size of loan constraints. A prudent approach would be to look at all of these, from each and every aspect, including your own ability to absorb the cost, the expected wait as a timeline, comply with the myriad documentation requirements, evaluate ability to meet review and diligence demands to boot, before taking the plunge. Not easy by any yardstick, but there are no short cuts. A little foresight and think-through at this stage will save you a lot of stress and heartburn ahead!!

3. **Costs and Sacrifices.** More than anything else, this is by and large the biggest pitfall that most promoters succumb to. The cost structures of banks especially, can be very complicated, and

need careful analysis. Apart from the usual interest on borrowings, which will remain dynamic with changes in the base rate, there may be costs on processing fees, documentation and compliance, stamp duty and legal costs, due diligence costs, annual renewal fees, service charges for special services, margin money for Letters of Credit and Bank Guarantees, to name a few. Each of these, needs to be baked into the costing to arrive at the fully loaded cost of the borrowing. The NBFCs are less cumbersome, but have their own standards, and their cost structures will include processing fees, EMIs, foreclosure charges, and a series of credit visits, evaluations and negotiations, to give you a flavour. This is apart from the cost of the expert, the lawyers, and the time of your accountants and CAs, working almost full time, on meeting the data requirements for the credit evaluation and other processes.

The other elements and sacrifices that it will demand will be in terms of time commitment for meetings, monthly reporting, re-negotiations with changes in your business environment, capital structure, management and team, and so on. In some cases, have seen bankers even have clauses which will require you to take their approval, before raising additional capital or making Board and Shareholding changes.

4. **Bankers and Their Obsessions.** Banking in India is driven by the philosophy of collateral-based lending. Their onus is always on ensuring they cover their exposure by way of collateral to the maximum extent possible. I have known Small Scale Enterprises where the ask has been as high as 75% collateral cover, on sanctioned limits. This is over and above your Balance Sheet and credit evaluation, as per their norms, meeting the risk criteria clearly. The second challenge you will encounter in their approach is the commitment to fund only 75% of your Current Assets, which is Inventory and Debtors, largely, with caveats. This has its genesis in the strong bias for manufacturing, on which their lending models originated. There would be a time limit for acceptable ageing for both these categories, usually limited to a maximum of 120 days. In cyclical businesses, or in challenging times, the propensity for inventory to build up, or debtors to accumulate, exceeding these limits of ageing, remains very high. Hence, part of both these Current Assets may become non-eligible for funding. This essentially means that their exposure to you by way of lending, is

restricted and more than protected, and these can put serious constraints on you. Think very long and hard, if you want to explore and consider the bankers' offer. Usually, as your business grows, your borrowing needs will grow, and if anything, the bank will only seek additional collateral, and not talk about releasing what they already have! Given the Fixed Assets trend, the value of that already provided would have fallen, remained flat or have a nominal appreciation, at best, and they would insist on additional cover, to provide for your aggressive growth projections and credit requirements. You must be prepared for a scenario where the collateral is likely to remain with the bank for a long time to come, until you find a buyer to takeover this debt as well! Doesn't sound very appealing, does it?

5. **The NBFC Dilemma.** The Non-banking Finance companies owe their existence to some of the pluses, in their ability to take credit risk, and profiles which the bankers are reluctant to touch, or consider taboo. Unfortunately, this differentiation has greyed, with the boundaries getting blurred. The NBFCs have also started seeking collateral for loans, not unlike the bankers, and at the same time hold onto their higher

pricing, stating higher risk taking and higher cost of capital for them. They still remain a good bet for smaller business loans, where they do lend without collateral. However, they have also tightened their screening and in most cases, need a track record of profitability of 3 years from the Organizations which seek to borrow. For you as a Start-up, this tends to become a stumbling block. The third pitfall that you will encounter, once you appreciate their method of lending, and recovery, is the concept of Equated Monthly Instalments. It essentially means you start paying back a part of the Principle (Borrowed amount) as well from day one. The loan is also made available to you for a smaller window, 3 years at best in most cases, while you keep paying back, essentially resulting in a smaller net borrowing as time progresses. In a growing business scenario, it would mean you may need to seek another loan to fund your future years' growth, or seek a top up loan from the same lender. Tedious, time consuming and adversely impacts your cash flows. Make sure you can deal with all of it, else side-step this option!

6. **Debt venture Funds and others.** The more recent development, Debt Funds are choices you may consider and evaluate as a route to

borrowings. Their pricing however, remains higher than the earlier two choices, given their risk appetites and their corpus available, along with the chunky exposures, which they seek. The process of approval and lending could be speedier, but the documentation, and the implications are far more complex and need detailed understanding. Individual lenders, HNIs, Family Offices, sometimes through private limited companies, are also choices that do come up. In all these cases, a due diligence of antecedents, reference and experience of other borrowers is advisable, and must be undertaken. Dubious reputations, attitudes, intentions are all in play in this space, in our country. Caution and adequate diligence are mandatory. Tread very carefully here!

7. **Trade-offs & Implications.** In essence, in any debt deliberations and evaluations, you will need to take a long term and holistic perspective to the transaction. It is never only about the borrowing and repayment capability. That is paramount, but there are other fallouts which are pitfalls that one needs to be wary of too. The obligation and collateral protection, the ability to return this asset, if at all, will be something your conscience

needs to deal with. The impact on cash flows and balance sheet health, will mean a new factor in your future initiatives of Fund Raising. Customer vendor ratings, their perception and comfort in dealing with you, suppliers and partners and their ability to take exposures, will all have impact and ramifications, which you may or may not be able to picturize or anticipate. The fine print of these agreements to borrow, and restrictive clauses there, can at times tie you down from even raising capital, let alone consider a sale and exit option to an interested, strategic acquirer. All these are realities that are rampant; there are innumerable Ventures who have burnt their fingers by succumbing to these pitfalls. There are no free lunches anyway, and a serious and long think is called for, before you decide to dive in! The choice is yours of course; do so after clearly evaluating the risks and potential pitfalls too.

8. **Paybacks and Exits.** While all of what is mentioned above is true, however, the fact remains that debt always comes at a lower cost vis-à-vis Equity, unless you are borrowing under extreme duress! Equity remains the most expensive of Capital options, and a balance in most businesses is prudent and pragmatic. Exiting borrowings are

easy in some cases, but more cumbersome in others. It is a factor that needs serious consideration and should weigh in on your decision to borrow, and sources of borrowing. The NBFC borrowings are normally the easiest to get out of; it is inherent to the nature of their business to complete one loan and close the documentation and move on to the next. That works in your favour, as their processes are fairly streamlined, and easier to comply with than most. Banks have it in their DNA to try and hold onto you as a borrower for as long as possible, and hence an exit is always an antithesis for them. They will do their best to hold on, if you have been paying their interest consistently and regularly. Other options will have easier exit clauses too, which you may use to make it happen. Your own internal practices and processes are also at times, a pitfall than can stymie your effort to clear your debt. The propensity to consider the debt as capital available to you, and hence use it to pay better to vendors, suppliers and partners, and extend credit facilities to customers, becomes a way of life, as the pressures on growth and revenues ramp up. Under these circumstances, even the thought of payback becomes wishful thinking!

In the chaotic and frantic world of your venture in your early days, the challenge of understanding, appreciating, evaluating and dealing with, the process of Debt or Borrowings for business, can be a very daunting and threatening prospect. All the more reason for you, to ensure you seek and get help and expertise, to walk you through this minefield of pitfalls and challenges.

Seek an expert and their opinion, before you, as Promoters, commit yourself to the debt burden. The small print of the contracts, the implications of the clauses in the sanction letter, the hidden and fully loaded costs, are all aspects that need complete understanding and appreciation.

Even at the end of it all, the impact on your Balance Sheet, its effect on your ability to raise capital going forward, meeting minimum criteria for Balance Sheet size, Net Worth of the Company, and health for new contracts, are all worth understanding, deliberating and digesting completely. It is never only about the cost of the debt, and its size and longevity. Taking an informed and pragmatic decision, is what prudence dictates, after assimilating all nuances and angles. Once convinced, take the plunge with glee!!

Chapter 11

THE ENTREPRENEURS' REALITIES

Too close to the action, a know-it-all syndrome, Bias for action overwhelms, perspective shortcomings, Playing hero or martyr, passion trumps rational thought, larger than the Enterprise, living only in the day, softer aspects take a back seat, Spreading too thin…

"We are not pulling our weight, and I am not at all pleased with this." Seema, the CEO and Co-Founder of the NativArts Handicrafts, yelled animatedly, as she banged the table with her fist.

"I do not understand what the rest of the team is doing, Sumer", this addressed to her Co-Founder and COO of their venture.

"Why does it take forever to do what I ask for? We are missing out on the demand for our products in this gifting and festive season. Am I to do everything myself?" she continued her rant.

"There have been serious disruptions in the supply chain and logistics, thanks to the monsoon and the damage to roads and connectivity. This had resulted in supply delays from our sourcing hubs." Sumer countered, in a very sober manner.

"Don't tell me that. There are alternate routes and ways to get them to our warehouses. You forget that I have lived and experienced this for the past 3 years." Seema reminded Sumer.

"Labour availability and productivity at our production centres from where we source, have got impacted too. Delayed harvesting, damaged crops has meant some of them have had severe strain in their farms. They have had to chip in there as well. That is the ground reality we have to take into account." Sumer again offered a perspective and reality check.

"We have to also relook at our pay outs to them, as they are dealing with damage to their venues, their labour camps and residences, in the aftermath of the floods and damage. May need to advance some more funds to help them tide over." This from Venkat, the CFO and third co-founder.

"Not our problem, Venki. Our focus has always been to deliver on our commitments and I have committed delivery of these consignments to our dealers this week. We have to make it happen," said Seema, her overbearing tone and manner not going unnoticed.

Venki and Sumer looked at each other and exchanged a resigned look.

"Seema, we are all going to look bad, if we default on our delivery commitments, but sometimes, factors are beyond our control. We need to possibly communicate this upfront in all honesty to the network." Sumer again, butting in, hoping to get her to see reason and the fact of the matter.

"We need to also think of our suppliers and carry them along, by empathising and supporting them in these times" he added further.

"We can raise some short-term debt to tide over the resultant cash flow pressures. I can work that out in a few days, if we agree to go ahead." Venki offered.

"Do you think we are successful and cash rich as a venture, that we can start thinking about everyone else ahead of our own immediate needs? We need to first think of ourselves. I do not have time for this. Sumer, you need to fix this, so get going. Do whatever it takes, but get the goods here in time."

With a finality and flourish, she stomped out of the meeting room, leaving both Sumer and Venkat, with a growing sense of concern and discomfort, and a very distinct foreboding of a disaster around the corner!

Again, a reality that often transpires in most early-stage Enterprise meeting rooms. The journey of the past few years, the trials and tribulations, the stress and tensions, the pace and complexity had all contributed and impacted all of them in myriad ways. Each one, had grown as a consequence, but had also got pushed into behaviours and personal afflictions, which reared its head in this meeting.

As you evolve as an enterprise, it impacts each one of you too, and the biggest challenge is for your personal growth to happen parallelly. It gives the venture and the business the maturity, depth and leadership it needs to transit to the next phase as an Organization. This personal growth, however, is fraught with pitfalls that you need to be conscious about, and guard yourself against.

Let's look at some of what Seema in particular, has succumbed to, and look for the pointers and red flags.

1. **Too close to the Action.** A natural outcome of living and breathing the Venture day in and out, this is the first behaviour trait you need to be conscious of. Your umbilical cord to the business,

tends to blindside you to some obvious errors and lacunae that exist in the product, processes and service standards. These, most times, will be internal and an obvious consequence of an evolving and growing Organization. However, there are a few occasions, when this may be external and beyond one's control. The flood situation that Seema was witnessing is just one such example. A detached and unbiased view would have helped her see what was obvious to all the others. This was an unprecedented and uncontrollable event, which had genuinely affected the supply chain of the Enterprise. However, her proximity and emotional involvement with the business has handicapped her, and she is unable to see it for what it really is. This is called emotional blinkers, and often leads you to miss the obvious pitfalls. Her ranting, and taking it out on everyone in the system, if continued in the same vein, will end up not only giving her hypertension, but also demoralizing the team, and lead to far-reaching unwanted consequences. Be conscious of this distinct possibility, and seek a third person's point of view from time to time, to negate this bias. Please show the maturity, and do try to distance yourself from the action, and see things for what they are. Do not let your emotional filters lead you astray. Don't miss the woods for the trees.

2. **The 'Know it all' Syndrome.** Often the fallout of being too attached to the idea and the venture once again, it slowly develops into a 'know it all' behaviour. You start thinking and believing, that there could be nothing about the business and venture that you could possibly be unaware of. This shows itself as deprecating comments, and brushing off any thought that others may have, as unworthy and downright stupid. Sometimes, it manifests itself as a castigating, "don't teach me" stance, which Seema was subtly demonstrating in the incident above. Once you succumb to this, you will deprive yourself of a holistic and pragmatic view of happenings; it may probably lead you to either bark up the wrong tree, or far worse, punish the messenger, and isolate yourself from the team in the bargain. No matter how long we have spent in the business and the industry, we can never start believing that we know everything there is to know. Such delusions can only lead to debacles! Even stalwarts, who have spent three decades and more in the industry cannot honestly make this claim! So, unlikely that you, with a few years under the belt, would have that, isn't it?

3. **Bias for Action Overrides all.** Remain conscious and watchful for this to rear its head. It will, at some stage in the journey, as the need to get multiple things actioned at the same time, is a given in an early-stage environment. With time, it becomes second nature for you as founders of the venture, to constantly need to take charge and get things done yourself. This 'activity syndrome', obscures the reality that there are times when you need to sit back, and take stock and observe, before you jump in, and start pulling all levers, and pushing buttons. A little bit of analysis and thought, will always enable the decision making, and the consequent action is likely to be more effective and efficient. Else you could fall victim to this Bias for Action, irrespective of consequences, which can have major, far reaching, adverse fallouts for the Venture. I am sure all of you would have had a distinct feeling, that possibly Seema was on the verge of asking Sumer, to personally go and get the stock loaded in vehicles and drive them in! Such foolishness, is the pitfall you need to protect yourself against.

4. **Perspective Shortcomings.** One reality, which will stand you in good stead, is the fact that as the Venture grows, it is not humanly possible to have

all the information, knowledge and perspective to do unilateral decision making. Seeking opinions, views, information, inputs and alternate perspectives from your Co-Founders, Employees, Partners, Customers and even Investors and Mentors, will help you greatly enhance your own, which is something you need more than you can imagine, as you build your Enterprise. Accepting that you do not know, is the first mantra, that will make you receptive to the fact there can be alternate views and opinions, about all that you think you see and hear. This will go a long way, in making you more grounded, pragmatic and open in your dealings and decisioning, and demonstrate your balance and maturity to all concerned.

5. **Playing a Hero or Martyr.** Don't let the early days, and the associated, unrelenting pressure and stress, make you start believing that the whole responsibility, in fact the whole world, rests on your shoulders. Do not succumb to playing Atlas, a disastrous pitfall to avoid, at all costs. Most promoters, do get caught up in the action and the Venture so much, that the obsession with it, begins to translate into this unwelcome behaviour. You start in all honesty, believing that you have to be the hero to the rescue in every situation, or

carry the burden of the venture solely on your shoulders! A dangerous self-fulfilling prophecy, as it will make you behave more and more as one, and start treating your Co-Founders and colleagues, as people whom you need to protect, rescue and carry, all by yourself. It tends to make people around you, stop taking ownership and pulling their own weight, and pass the monkey onto you! You definitely don't want that to happen, as it often leads to the creation of a very disinterested and demotivated, team and Organization. Over time, it also manifests itself in a very directional and dictatorial style of leadership, which in an early-stage Venture, with Co-Founders and committed employees, often goes against organization building, and creates an imploding environment. It's becomes a bomb waiting to go off, with a possibly disastrous collapse of the venture.

6. **Passion Trumps Rational Thinking.** Unbridled passion can at times be self-destructive. However, every Start-up is driven by the passion of the Founders, primarily, in the early stages. This paradox is a given, and you need to keep it in mind always. The Venture is often like an engine running on adrenaline, fuelled by the passion which each one of you brings to the table. You

need to be wary and guard against the downside of this behaviour. It often unfortunately translates into a situation where you start using passion as the answer to every problem. If there is a crisis, if we are passionate enough, we will solve it! If there are floods, my passion will enable me to navigate the flood waters, and somehow get the goods to my warehouse! The pitfall here is that rationality and the complete perspective, is sometimes lost under the deluge of passion, and its unrelenting barrage. Do remember, that passion gets you that extra edge, but can never substitute the resources and support required. It cannot be the only factor to execute. Be conscious of this trait making its presence felt in your actions, and step back often to re-examine the challenge from a finite distance, with rational think.

7. **Larger than the Enterprise.** This is one huge misconception, that takes root not only with Promoters and Founders, but even amongst the early set of employees! In early stages, the working of the venture does depend completely on a few members, and as growth transpires, it helps create a great sense of achievement and ownership, amongst those that were part of the journey thus far. However, in some cases, this starts to

grow into maniacal proportions at times, and the individuals slowly start believing that the venture cannot survive without them. Ergo, I am larger than the Enterprise, and it cannot exist without me! Please keep your eyes, ears, and minds open to catch this egoistic manifestation early, in your employees and yourself too!! The first signs of this is usually by way of flexing of muscles to break ranks and discipline, flaunting rules and processes, under the smug assumption that your self-perceived stature, gives you the liberty to do so. This is disruptive and destructive behaviour, especially from the leaders, and can easily push the Organization on a downward spiral of implosion and waste. Nip all such thoughts and actions in the bud. Confront this behaviour; counsel, talk through, even castigate and pull up if necessary, to clear the air and reset the thinking. Be the harshest on your own self; critically examine every action and behaviour of yours, actively seek feedback, and remain ever vigilant that this does not rear its head. Use your Co-Founders, Mentors, Advisors as sounding boards to check if you are demonstrating this trait, in any form or manner, in all that you are doing, on a day-to -day basis. You may not even be aware of it, or sense it, given the fact that you are constantly swamped with activity and decisions, in these early stages.

8. **Living only by the Day.** Please be wary of what I call the 'activity syndrome', a propensity to only live with activities on a day-to-day basis, and rarely stop to do some medium and long term thinking for the Venture. In the early days, more than ever, it is critical you are conscious of this. The stress of getting things going, managing all the elements with a skeleton crew, normally creates an ideal environment for you to quickly settle into this default mindset. Your day is so swamped with activity, that your mind gets filled with all of these, and leaves very little space and thought for anything else! It slowly develops as a defence mechanism, as you keep telling yourself, let me go through this day, and not worry about tomorrow, next week, next month or next year. You dread going there, as you are reluctant to open that door, fearful of the probably depressing scenarios that may unfold. Don't succumb to this pitfall; it is possibly a given that it will show itself in your journey at various points in time. It will call for all your maturity and balance, to push back and keep it in abeyance. One pragmatic and practical way of possibly dealing with this, is to schedule

regular meetings with your Mentor or Advisor, with the only agenda as medium and long-term thinking for the Enterprise. Dwell on the possible scenarios that could unfurl, and the solutions that the Venture may need, to deal with it. Alternate plans and actions should be thought through, discussed and stored, for future reference and implementation. This will ensure the dread that is subconsciously there, will start to get addressed, and consequently shrink and hopefully vanish.

9. **Softer Aspects take a Back Seat.** Another serious lacuna and a huge pitfall to avoid, is the propensity to push to the background the softer aspects of the business and venture. Be it counselling, feedback sessions, goal setting and brainstorming for the future, interpersonal issues and confrontations, and their redressal, career growth and development discussions. They are all victims, and the outcome of the activity syndrome, amongst other things. Seema did give some indication of her mindset, in the opening conversation, if you remember. It is critical you set aside time, find time and give it due attention and importance, while juggling the challenges and crises that keep coming up with unrelenting frequency. It is obviously convenient to relegate this softer and often time-consuming

issue, to way down the priority list for yourselves, as Founders and leaders of the venture. However, the implications of doing so can be disastrous. It is in the early days, that the team and its members, will need far more reassurance, comfort, direction, mentoring, hand holding and perspective, which they would expect from you, and look up to you for. Neglect this at your own risk!!

10. **Spreading Yourself too Thin.** The propensity to try version 2.0 of your product or service, enter new markets and segments, create new disruptive products, will all show itself as you start seeing some traction and success with your first offering, in the Venture. While there is no question of the need to constantly innovate for new products and improve offerings, while developing alternative markets, to keep the growth and progress going, the word of caution here is to keep in mind that you do not spread yourself too thin. It can have a telling effect on you, the team and your resources, and may in fact sabotage the growth and stabilization of the first product and offering!

It will call for pulling yourself back, showing maturity and balance, as you think through any such exercise. Do exercise adequate caution and thinking, before you jump into any such expansion plans, and bounce off such thoughts with your Mentors and Advisors too, before embarking on an aggressive expansion journey. This prudence will pay off and ensure that you don't jeopardize the good run that you may have established thus far for the venture.

Your role as a Founder of a Start-up will evolve very quickly from an adventurer to an Organization builder, developer, mentor, coach, and a true leader, once you start the journey. This rapidly changing colours and hues of your role, will call for a parallel growth and maturing, of you as an individual and leader. It will necessitate tremendous amount of learning on your part, and imbibing concurrently, while executing, scaling and growing the business itself.

Never an easy task, and given the limited exposure and experience that you may have had in the past, will mean great stress, and a real challenge for you. Use your well-wishers, consciously, to help you negotiate and successfully deal with this true behemoth of a challenge. Make sure ego and pride are set aside, as this will be a revealing, and at times, painful journey, for you too! There are unfortunately, no short cuts to this.

Only you can, and will have to undertake, this demanding and challenging transition and growth journey for yourself, along with the journey of the Venture. Your success will be critical to the success of the venture, and synergistic growth is almost mandatory, and paramount to the ultimate growth and credibility of the Organization. Do give it its due.

Chapter 12

GENERIC PITFALLS TO AVOID

The Idea Obsession, The Profitability Syndrome, The Here & Now Fallacy, All Battles have to be Won, The Cost Cutting Paradox, The Control Fixation, Benchmarking Against Giants, The Efficiency Mindset, The sunk cost conundrum, Stretch without Capability…

The Offsite Meeting of the Health2Wealth Company, was in the middle of an animated discussion.

"Let's first accept that we have made serious errors in our journey so far, and it has cost us substantially", Anil, the CEO and Co-Founder of the Venture voiced, albeit with some remorse and regret.

"All my learnings from the past few years together, I have tried to capture, which I am tabling. Am open to debate and review that," he continued, after a pause.

The Enterprise had crossed the first set of growth hurdles, and was now poised for the next stage of growth. The first round of Capital had been raised, the team had been strengthened, cash flows had started coming in, and customer acquisition and retention was looking up substantially. Parallelly, processes had been piloted, reworked and streamlined, but the recent pandemic had put the brakes on this roller coaster ride.

The team was meeting after a long hiatus, now that the restrictions on hotel stays and small gatherings had been lifted, at an offsite location. The objective was to brainstorm and figure out ways and means of reworking their strategy to take into account the new realities of the marketplace. All 12 of them, the core team, were huddled together, with social distancing norms in place, for this purpose. Their mentor, Dr. Anupama, a seasoned and experienced professional, was also there to share her years of corporate and start-up wisdom. She was possibly the most qualified to do so, given her extensive work with Start-ups and Small & Medium Enterprises, after her successful stint as a healthcare professional, and as a CEO and Board Member, in the corporate world.

"We are not in any serious trouble given our area of operation, and health care products are only exploding, thanks to the pandemic and the awareness and focus it has generated." Sunita, the second Founder, and the COO of the Enterprise said, with a smile of satisfaction on her face.

"My point is not that, Sunita. I am trying to bring forth and table the fact that there have been serious generic lapses in our approach in the past, which have cost us quite a bit, in our journey thus far."

"I want us to ponder, digest and accept these errors in judgement and work out the strategies of how we will avoid these pitfalls going forward." Anil was setting the context for the meeting here.

Ramaswamy, the third Founder and the CFO, then chipped in, "One of my main observations and concerns is this. We have chased too many perfections, battled the competition with a need to win every time, and lost track of our costs and profitability objectives, in our obsession with the need to be one up on everyone else."

"Our financials have taken serious dents and hits, and we need to guard against this obsessive need to win always. Let's not forget that we do not have an endless horde of cash, nor can we raise it at the drop of a hat, to match the global giants," he concluded with finality.

"Our efficiencies are the best and we need to do what it takes to stay there. If it means extra costs, so be it. Remember, we are also doing it with the team we have with us, for the past two years."

"My opinion is that we did what was right, and it has paid off for us, in other ways," Sunita was quick to defend.

Anil again tried to get the discussion back on track, but knew he needed to now defer to the experience and judgement of Dr. Anupama, as they seemed to have hit an impasse.

"Doctor, can you throw some light on this? Are we wrong in thinking we need to look back, identify the pitfalls we have succumbed to, rectify our errors in ways, before we move ahead? Is this stock-taking and contemplation any use at all? We all seem to have our own fixed views on this".

A feeling of deja vu, I am sure a number of you will have. The long road to success, is laden with such pauses and introspection, and should be so, for the pitfalls that confront us are so diverse, disguised and diabolic, that we do end up succumbing to them, and enduring the pain, loss and regret, that they bring with them. A dispassionate analysis and understanding helps in correcting this bias, and better equips us to move ahead, to the next phase of the journey.

The business-related pitfalls, which tend to be very difficult to see, and hence easy to fall prey to, can often be grouped into certain generic categories, and here I seek to possibly identify some of those, with a few suggested pointers for dealing with them.

1. **The Idea Obsession.** The first of these, is an obsessive attachment and love for your business idea. As you move down the road towards building a successful business, this obsession can, and often does, push you into the pitfalls which it brings with it. It begins with you adhering to the scope of the idea to the T, and refusing to tweak, modify or pivot the product, service or execution, in keeping with environment changes, customer feedback and preferences, and new competitor offerings. If along with that, there are 'Black Swan' events, like the pandemic, to throw a spanner in the works, this obsessive behaviour can easily throw you off the road, into wilderness and decay. Stay watchful and mindful of this. The second manifestation it induces, is the reluctance to do anything which is different from the idea, even if there is a need and market opportunity staring at you in the face. It may be by way of an additional product,

a different channel of distribution, a new market and customer segment with a different end use, a completely different pricing and servicing strategy, rebranding and repositioning of the product or service; all of these are challenges that will confront you at various points in your journey. The key is to keep an open mind, and be pragmatic about being open to change, if your business realities demand it. The idea is just an idea, and it will need to be adapted and changed, for commercial success, keeping in mind the dynamic environment and market conditions. The truth of the matter is, the business and its success, is the end game, and the idea is only an element, or one of the factors for achieving it. Pragmatic thinking may even suggest pivoting to a completely different idea, in case of disruptive events or challenges. Be open to relooking at it contextually, and evaluate.

2. **The Profitability Syndrome.** Too much of an obsession with profitability is like missing the woods for the trees, especially in an early-stage venture. During the early days, the fact remains that the absolute profitability by way of margins, is not as contextually relevant as cash flows. A lower margin, but better and earlier inflows, is a logical trade-off, in a venture hard up for cash.

Managing the cash flows should be the number one priority of the Founders, till such time you can see a healthy bank balance, which can provide a long enough runway to the venture. A two years forward looking cash reserve is a good bench mark. Paradoxically, this is also the precise reason, not to undercut the price to an extent that it means a net negative cash flow, given the cost structures. The other manifestation one often sees in such Enterprises, is the short sightedness of missing out on quantum leaps of growth and annuity income, sacrificed at the altar of minimum profit margins. It is never a simple mathematical equation. These decisions need to be driven by a broader and longer-term perspective, and if need be, marginal costing, incremental revenues, services and other income, longevity of the revenue stream, and the trade-offs should all be carefully evaluated. Do not get bogged down by the profitability trap. The third pitfall under this generic category, is the foolhardy decision to raise prices to meet the minimum standards of profits set internally. The price that you can command is never driven by your internal cost structures and your margin expectations. It is controlled by market forces and what the customer perceives as the value for the product or service.

It is akin to raising the minimum qualifying time standards for the Olympics for our country participants, as we cannot produce athletes who can meet the international standards. That's just fooling yourself, to cater to your own profitability syndrome. Don't attempt to cut your nose to spite your face!!

3. **The Here and Now Fallacy.** Often, in our daily efforts to get our arms around the various challenges, and pitfalls that confront us, we tend to get caught in the 'Here and Now 'of things. The need to fix the issues, problems immediately, and move on, becomes a default behaviour of ours. This is a natural outcome of the strong bias for action that exists in the early days, and tends to envelop everything with time. Most of the issues and challenges which confront us, do call for some thought, review, feedback, data and independent opinions and views, before we can jump into a course-correction or rectification mode. As leaders of the venture, you, in particular, in particular will get drawn into this default option syndrome, and fall prey to this fallacy. It will manifest itself in impulsive off-the-cuff decisioning, opinions, responses, and even significant strategic changes, which is a harbinger of grief and regret to come.

Remain conscious of this, and set checks and balances for yourselves to prevent this from recurring, every time. A good self-restraint is the practice of taking a few minutes to confer amongst yourselves as Co-Founders, and have the discipline of ensuring decisions are not taken without this interaction. Can be simple WhatsApp or messaging based conversations as well. The other test is to ensure you keep asking yourselves what is the worst that would happen if there is a delay, or a wrong decision taken. This thought can help you better appreciate the degree of impact in terms of costs, time and resources. Some thinking on consequences will easily put things in perspective and improve the quality of decision making substantially. Please do remember, not taking a decision and deferring it, can, at times, be a decision in itself, and maybe the best one for the Enterprise!

4. **All Battles Have to be Won.** I hope you have seen early losses, and setbacks in your journey more than a few times; Helps keep your enthusiasm and optimism in check, while leading you safely through this minefield. It reiterates the fact that all battles need not be won. Often a fallout of the desire to confront challenges and push back with

self-belief. Over time, this confrontation approach, translates into a misplaced determination, that all battles and confrontations have to end in victory for you, and the venture. Stay clear of this trap! It tends to draw you and the team into lose-lose battles, do or die battles, and this journey is never about dying in battle. It is about negotiating, side stepping, avoiding, backing off, regrouping and returning to the fight once again! You may need to lose a few battles, to win the war for business success! The end goal of a successful enterprise, should be crystal clear to you as Founders. Use failures, as stepping stones and experience, and learn from it. Rejig, retool, rework your strategies, tactics and ploys to explore a different angle and side to attack or circumvent the problem or challenge. This destructive mindset, of the need to win all battles, tends to show itself in many colours and hues. The first is this adamant streak of never backing off and continued confrontation. It could be competition, investors, the board, suppliers and their associations, resellers and supply chain members, even employees and well-wishers! Don't get drawn into this, and use a reality check and sounding board to alert you of this, when it happens. The unfortunate truth is that you are often blind to it, and a voice of reason and restraint is necessary to ensure you do not fall into these manholes. The second is this innate tiresome attitude of not letting go, and endlessly extending meetings and discussions, until you have won your argument and everyone endorses your point of view. It creates what is known as 'intellectual fatigue', and people give up fighting or arguing, but do not necessarily agree to your point of view. This will lead to teams, often not being committed to the actions decided, and result in diffused efforts and sub-optimal outcomes. In the long run, it can easily translate into the entire Organization becoming a team of yes men, just toeing the line! The value of a diverse, well-rounded, competent and knowledgeable team, is lost to the venture and you, as their leaders, in the bargain.

5. **The Cost Cutting Paradox.** Your journey will have inflexion points, where you may need to tighten your belts, take some hard calls, push back on often seemingly desirable spends, to keep the engine running, and last out the tough times. This phase, often puts us in a dilemma as the ability and propensity to take these calls, is clouded by emotion, passion, nostalgia, and personal preferences. This biased decisioning may result in

creating more problems, than addressing some! There will be hesitation, regret, turmoil, sitting on the fence, delaying tactics, which will all manifest; you are but a human being and not infallible. The harsh fact of the matter is that it will need to be done, and you will have to bell the cat, being the Founders. The paradox lies in the fact that when things are bleak, you may have to take this step, and it will leave you with a feeling of being unfair, as akin to kicking a person when they are down. I have seen this closely in this pandemic, when tough calls had to be taken by Ventures, under duress. Everyone does not necessarily get it right, even if they manage to bite the bullet, and go ahead with it. To deal with it, you will have to tighten your girdles, and follow a principle of musts versus needs, i.e. any element of the cost which is critical to the continued operations of the Venture, to the delivery of the product or service to the customer, and which is intrinsic to this core process, should be left alone and protected. All others are, to put it bluntly, nice to have and dispensable. It will mean employees too; the teeth of the Organization, if functional and delivering, should be weighed differently from the tail, which is the backend and support structure. However, you may end up setting off a chain reaction of low morale, fear and mistrust, insecurities and irrational behaviour, all leading to furthering the downward spiral in the business too. Open and honest communication, accepting your handicap and inability to sustain the cost structures, explaining the need and rationale, will help in softening the impact and easing the panic levels. Think long and hard, before taking these calls, and options like compensation cuts, conversion to variable pay, your own personal compensation cut or kept in abeyance, extended credit terms to vendors and suppliers, changes in credit policies for customers to collect upfront, are all on the table for you. You need to assess the likely impact, and pick the ones with the lowest long-term consequences. What you may need to guard against however, is not to cut so close that you bleed to death as a business. These are unfortunately, also times when you may need investments to pivot your business process, product or service, to work around the revised reality. Please evaluate such investment differently, and do categorise them in the 'must haves,' bucket. My suggestion would be to make sure you lean on your mentors and advisors, seek their ratification and endorsement, before taking the plunge. Your being too close to the action, may blindside you from being rational and pragmatic!

6. **The Control Fixation.** As a Founder and promoter of the Venture, there will perpetually be an intensely felt need, to always be in charge and in control. Not because you want it, but because you falsely believe that if you lose control, there will be unbridled chaos, leading to the ultimate destruction of the Venture. As an individual, passionately and deeply involved with the business, it is human to succumb to this behaviour. So, contrary to what should be the logical approach, you may tend to get more and more dictatorial and tight-fisted about decisions, costs, investments, hiring and any interventions that the Venture may need. Instead of letting go, and using exception management to keep yourself in the thick of things, you may actually take away any leeway, for allowing executives, partners, employees or even your Co-Founders to do what they are possibly more knowledgeable, qualified and in the know, to rightfully do! Do guard against this disastrous propensity, as it can undo what years of good work and constructive team building has done. Learn to let go; do you see shades of martyr tendencies here too?

7. **Benchmarking Against Giants.** A trap, which you may get stuck in forever, if you walk into. Have often seen Entrepreneurs compare themselves to the multinational giants and benchmark against their productivity, costs, revenues, margins and returns, and give themselves and their teams sleepless nights, as an unfortunate consequence. You need to exercise abundant caution and thought, before you start getting wedded to these criteria or 'standards' of performance evaluation. You will end up short-changing yourself and your team in the bargain. The fact remains that at various stages of business growth, these parameters will necessarily look different. Revenue per employee, cost of acquisition, overheads as percentage of revenue, productivity and efficiency criteria, gross margin per employee, profit per employee, are all factors which change hues at each stage of growth. These numbers in a mature and steady-state company, will show up differently, versus a small and rapidly growing venture. Foolhardy to penalise yourself and the team for something which is intrinsic to the stage where the venture is, in the business growth cycle! Blindly pushing yourself to meet the benchmarks set by these large, mature establishments, will end up

being counter-productive, and often frustrating to the team, as they may appear unattainable. It can adversely impact morale, and in turn, lower efficiency and productivity, significantly. While being paranoid and closely tracking other players is perfectly understandable, and even desirable, an unreasonable obsession with such benchmarking, is a pitfall you definitely need to save yourself from!

8. **The Efficiency Mindset.** As the business starts to mature and settle down into a good rhythm and a healthy growth rate, after a couple of years, and the numbers start to kick in, one of the mindsets that you need to be watchful for, is the Efficiency Mindset. The impulse and propensity is often to settle into a comfort zone, and seek to extract value with efficiencies of costs, Investments and people, as these tend to appear as low hanging fruits. However, the Venture at that time, is still in a rapid growth phase, and the expansion into new markets and segments is as yet on the drawing board, most times. The belief that you have reached a scale and size, and it calls for seeking incremental gains, tending to milk efficiencies, is the pitfall you need to guard against. It takes a fairly long time for the business to hit steady-state, which is when

seeking efficiencies and tweaking costs and efforts, are ploys to be used and adapted extensively. It is not a medium-term ploy or tactic; your Enterprise is still learning, adapting, retooling, innovating, pivoting, and experimenting. These times are meant for an effectiveness mindset, which keep the venture agile, open and willing to learn and change. You, as the leaders, have to ensure the mindset stays in this zone, and does not lapse into the efficiency mindset. May seem very counter intuitive, but is the way to go! Don't get lulled into the belief that you have arrived, a little too early. Stay hungry and paranoid, to survive and thrive, in the long term.

9. **The Sunk Cost Conundrum.** The journey to growth, profitability and success is fraught with challenges, pitfalls and even dead-ends. As you learn to negotiate these, it will call for experimenting and piloting ideas, products, thoughts, processes, all with the end objective of overcoming these hurdles that confront you. There are clearly no free lunches and short cuts, and hence investment in terms of capital, resources, people and time, are a given. Often these end up being lost to the cause, as the interventions do not always deliver the goods. These failures

will tend to work on your mind, as you try and juggle the cash flows and demands of the business to continue to survive, revive and thrive, in the aftermath of these setbacks and shocks. I have often seen Founders, while navigating this, fall into the Sunk Cost Conundrum. Your thinking tends to get biased with the costs of the failed experiments and efforts, and the decisions you take going forward, start to get influenced by this. "We have already put X Thousand Dollars into this. We must make this work" tends to become the refrain, from you to the team. That precisely, is the pitfall! If you start letting the costs of your earlier failures, weigh in and influence the next set of decisions you take, as an important factor, you have succumbed to the Sunk Cost Conundrum. You may end up, pushing a failing idea, or an ill-conceived execution, instead of cutting your losses and moving on, as a consequence. Whereas, a zero-based decisioning, starting ab initio, will easily tell you to drop the obviously ill-conceived attempt, and move on. It may show up in people decisions too; "We have spent so much time and money training and developing this person. We should try and get them up the curve and guide them to become more effective." You have to keep the sunk costs aside, and take the decision whether the individual has potential, and is worth retaining and counselling to get better, and not because you spent significant sums of money on them! There will be similar experiences with suppliers, designs, products, services, partners, channels, campaigns, marketing initiatives, the list can go on! Have witnessed Ventures get taken down this path, with disastrous outcomes, as promoters have fallen for this conundrum. Step with extreme caution, and ask yourself constantly if you are letting any sunk cost concerns, influence every unique decision that you are likely to take.

10. **Stretch without Capability.** The law of elasticity says that there is a finite limit to the capability of stretching a piece of metal, rubber, string, or anything else you can think of! It is driven by their capability to absorb the stretch. Please add people, processes, resources and ideas to the list! The early days in a Start-up is a period of stretch for everything, and the propensity to do so, is justified and called for on your part. But the pitfall to avoid is to assume that the limits to the stretch is infinite! As the leader, the onus is on you to keep monitoring and tracking the responses to the stretch, and arrive at a capability limit for

every element, human, equipment, process and parameter you are dealing with. Make sure you do not push it beyond this, as the consequences will not do any good for you in the long run. You will have to accept the fact that you may need to replace, modify, enhance, upgrade, redesign, rework some or all of these, at various stages of the growth cycle of the Enterprise. It is a harsh reality that there may come a stage in the Organizations journey, when even you as the Founders, may not be the right individuals to continue to lead the Organization, and may need to be replaced! Remember this and keep your antennae up for signs and indications, which tell you it may be time to bite the bullet on a few components, for the larger good of the Venture!

All of these generic pitfalls, are what you are likely to encounter as you start the scaling up journey of your Venture. They are generic because they manifest themselves in different ways and tend to confound, confuse and compel you to make errors of judgement, with far reaching repercussions. Be wary of these, seek independent feedback, and keep looking at yourself in the mirror, to reassure yourself you are not falling prey to these.

Your mentors, advisors, senior teammates, are good sounding boards, as are your co-founders, well-wishers and even family. It is true that often, these flaws in your thinking are easily visible to people who are observing you from the vantage point of being uninvolved, and thus, objective and unbiased with their observations. A little humility and acceptance of the fact that you are fallible, and a likely prey to these, will stand you in good stead and enable you to safely and successfully, negotiate this minefield of pitfalls and challenges!

Chapter 13

CONCLUDING THOUGHTS

Scaling up a venture is a Balancing Act, Strategy and Thinking Ahead is key, Process and People Investments a Must, Setting the Pace & Drive is a Given, Cash Flows Drive the Ability to Grow, Pricing and Credit Terms Critical, Vision and Hunger to Succeed are key ingredients, Regulations and Compliance need constant Watch, Teeth to Tail Ratios require Constant Calibration, Cash Breakeven an Essential Milestone, Personal Growth Must keep Pace…

As I now come to the close of my earnest attempt to present, my experiences and learnings, from my journey with start-ups and early-stage Ventures over the past decade and more, there are some other thoughts that come to mind, that should rightfully have a place in this narrative.

These are all encompassing, crossing lines of functions, roles & time-frames to earn a prominent place at the back of your minds. These guidelines or pointers, can act as beacons, to help you successfully navigate this challenging maze of a journey, as you scale the venture, which remains close to your heart.

They are random thoughts; in no particular order or sequence, and their relative importance is for you to ascertain and assign. I have reason to believe that each one of them deserves to be here, as part of your key takeaways from this book, that you have hopefully read, contemplated upon, and digested.

Hope they stand you in good stead in your journey, as you focus on building a successful enterprise.

1. **Scaling up a Venture is a Balancing Act.** Critical to keep this perspective, in anything you do as you go about building the business. There will always be diverse, distinct and often conflicting priorities and pulls, at logger heads, striving for your immediate attention and action. Decision making will always be a challenge, as you balance out the pros and cons, of the opposing factors and elements that scream for attention. Each one of them, will appear urgent and important, and often threaten your peace of mind with

conflicting views and data. Keep walking the middle path, weighing the various factors and elements constantly, reprioritizing, recalibrating, reassessing and rearranging them in your own unique journey, as the dynamic environment and market forces, play their part in creating, at times, tectonic shifts. The need to balance frugality with prudent investments, hiring with strategic outsourcing, aggression with adequate caution, short-term activities with long-term thinking, empowerment with monitoring and control, expansion with strategic pruning, is a given, and a must! There is almost nothing that will be a simple no brainer; don't look for it and anything that appears so, is too good to be true! Brace yourself for this balancing act throughout the journey.

2. **Strategy and Thinking Ahead is Key.** Though never easy, or simple, it is however advisable to strategize and co-ordinate all your actions keeping the ultimate purpose and goal in mind. Take time and think through possible scenarios in the times to come, and the various options and plans available to you, to be able to deal with it. The need to be proactive and prepared cannot be overstated. As founders, you need to set aside

time during each day, for this critical exercise. A quiet period, when the chaos has not yet warmed up for the day, or has wound down for the day, is ideally suited for this. Seek and use all help you can get. Advisors, mentors, support groups, best practice shares, investors, and anything else you can think of, are all in play, and often good sounding board and thought provocateurs. It helps you prepare and better deal with the pitfalls and challenges that rear their heads, from time to time. Winging it, is never the best option, as it often tends to result in a loss of control, and invariably letting the problems overwhelm you, thus put you under severe stress. It can easily lead to decision fatigue, where you lose the ability to take balanced decisions, which are detrimental to the enterprise. It can stress you further, as you realize the errors, and in extreme cases, end in a depressed mind!

3. **Process and People Investments a Must.** An early implementation of these two will go a long way in keeping your venture on even keel, and enable you to survive every challenge and pitfall you encounter. Take the time and trouble, to define the processes that will be followed for every product or service delivery initiative, apart from the internal

discipline measures as well! It may seem very trivial and an overkill to start with, but it helps identify possible areas of stress and failure, as well as highlight the need for technology interventions, which may otherwise evade you. A detailed think through and planning exercise, has benefited most start-ups who can look back with satisfaction at the progress they have managed to achieve. Identify key resource and knowledge gaps, and plug them in too, by finding and hiring the right talent and capability. A mapping and even a diagrammatic representation, will also throw light on these gaps and the needs. It will enable you as founders, to transit from activity management to process review and control, an essential step in a growing enterprise. The reason I have deliberately labelled them as investments, is the fact that if you make the error of seeing them as costs, you may tend to get swayed by the need for frugality and ignore or defer these much-needed Investments in the early stage. Be selective, and exercise all caution and care, in identifying these, but once done, please bite the bullet and put in the technology, people and processes which are critical and necessary, to make things happen in an effective and scalable manner!!

4. **Cash Flows Drive the Ability to Grow.** For some time to come, in your Business journey, the fact will remain that cash-flows need to be the pivot around which your decision making is driven, and not profits. Healthy and positive cash-flows, will allow you the liberty and discretion to push for growth, be it by way of more inventory, product range, people to execute, alternate service models, differential pricing, alternate distribution channels, marketing initiatives, and pilot projects for future expansion of business. Track it, monitor it, control it, rationalise it, like a hawk, and do not take your eye off this ball! Cash in the bank will also let you sleep easier, keep you on a healthy even keel, and in turn make the quality of your interactions with the team, far more motivating and energising, as a consequence. The reality is that in the growth journey, there will be curve balls that will get thrown at you, and it is critical you are prepared to deal with that, which a healthy balance and predictable cash flow position, makes easier. This will contribute in enabling you to take decisions unfettered by the fear of falling short in funding it. This is apart from the fact that, it puts you in a better

position to negotiate with investors, bankers, suppliers, partners, even potential new hires for that matter! It improves your ability to hold out and push back, in all these negotiations, and not give in to unreasonable demands and clauses, which are likely to adversely impact the venture. Intense and drawn-out efforts are often needed to ensure a win-win for all. While lower profits are par for the course, in the early growth stages, continued bleeding and burning of this valuable commodity, will raise eyebrows, and tempt the sharks and exploiters too.

5. **Pricing and Credit Terms Critical.** Your two drivers of the business, Revenues and costs, are largely dependent on the pricing and price negotiations you have with your suppliers, partners and customers. The second, but even more critical element, cash-flow, is driven by the credit terms you offer, or manage to negotiate. As founders, my advice to you would be to keep yourself on top of these two elements, in great detail, across the various diverse interactions where they are involved. Hence, rental negotiations, compensations structures for hires, purchase agreements for the office or business, pricing and payment terms for customer segments, channel

margins and settlements, marketing spends and payment cycles, raw material procurement and terms, technology and capital purchases, are all areas where in the initial stages, you need to be in the know and on top of decisions that are being taken, which are of significance to the enterprise. You may define boundaries within which it will not require your intervention, to empower key employees. However, beyond these limits, the decision has to come to you. Do not fall into the trap of laisse faire, and let things happen in the flow. If you let it slide, the damage it can do before you are able to correct it, will be almost irrecoverable, more so in the early stages. Do not slacken your focus on this aspect of the business, irrespective of the fires and chaos around you!!

6. **Vision & Hunger to Succeed are critical Ingredients.** Have a clear vision of what and where you want the venture to be, in the medium and long-term. There is nothing like a clear focus, to drive synergy and teamwork towards a common goal. Share the same with one and all, as often as possible, as pointed out earlier, and keep recalibrating this, as time moves on. It helps to keep the constant changes and reworking of processes, products and services, on track, and

ensures it does not result in unrelated, disjointed and mis-directed efforts! This obviously, also needs to be fuelled by the hunger to succeed; an unquenchable fire in the belly, that keeps you and the enterprise going. If Vision is the destination, hunger is the fuel to keep the engine going to get you there. If either one of them is missing or weak, it often results in an 'also ran', as a venture. Keep moving the bar up, as you drive the organization towards the end goal, creating stretch milestones, which are a steep ask, but not impossible!! A razor-sharp focus on an end goal, and an unrelenting drive is a combination that works, and are critical components for success.

7. **Regulations & Compliance need Constant Watch.** The economic, political, social and regulatory environment are other key aspects that form part of the ecosystem that your start-up has taken birth in. The market dynamics and customer behaviour, which drive the business goals are the core and genesis of your idea taking on business contours. However, they only serve to fuel and enable the desire to convert the idea to a venture, and is akin to giving birth. These other elements, are the factors which are instrumental for longevity, and influence whether it survives,

revives and thrives, as it blossoms into adulthood. The fact remains that the regulatory framework and its evolution, is a culmination of all the above elements working in tandem, and hence, the cornerstone of the watch list for you! Though bitter but the truth, is the fact that your venture needs to navigate the maze of regulations, their compliance requirements, and their subtle nuances of classification, that is not only confusing, but often deliberately so!! Avoiding the pitfalls of non-compliance and regulatory non-conformance, is paramount for you as founders, as it ensures you are left alone to do what you need to, to nurture and grow the enterprise. These are also undergoing rapid changes, driven by economic, global and political considerations. A momentary slip, can often lead to a long and tedious journey of constant retribution, needlessly creating operating handicaps, which you can do without. Keep it on top of your priority list, and ensure you are compliant, always, and in time. It will save you many heartburns and sleepless nights!! Please use your Chartered Accountants as your navigators for these treacherous waters, as they do have the experience and knowledge, to guide your efforts in the right direction!!

8. **Teeth to Tail Ratios require Constant Calibration.** An unfortunate but often occurring phenomena is the inability of leaders of start-ups to show the right balance and presence of mind, as they build their teams, to guard against making the organization 'Tail heavy'. In the early stages, the fact remains that you are always hard up for hiring and staffing, and the need to make do with less manpower than desirable, is a given. In this scenario, there will always be demands on resourcing from both the Business Development and Sales teams, and the Operations and Delivery teams. You will often have to pick and choose who to satisfy, and who you will deny. The easy and less unsettling way out, is to agree to the staffing for the office, as more often than not, you as the founding CEO, are personally driving the front end, and can push the front-end team, to accept the haircut. You do not want to be seen by the rest of the organization, as hogging the resources. You invariably tend to err on the safe side, and this gradually results in the teeth-to-tail ratio, getting completely skewed towards the back end. More often, with layering and large control spans, while the front end remains lean and mean, which is how the entire structure

needs to be!! Keep recalibrating constantly, and guarding against this behaviour. It's a pitfall that creeps up on you. Downsizing in the back end, is often more painful and damaging to the morale of the enterprise, as it is more visible, and more noticeable and significant, thanks to the fat accumulated. My advice here would be, question every hire, especially managers and above, which is layering at its best. They often add very little incrementally to the venture in value, especially in the earlier stages of rapid growth. Let the tail stay behind the curve of requirement, and focus on the teeth, to give yourself more engine power for revenues and customer acquisition. It is better that you are confronted by the problem of fulfilment, rather than the challenge of finding new customers and growth opportunities. There is no fulfilment anyway, without orders to fulfil. It is prudent to remember that Business Growth is the cause for delivery capability enhancement, and not vice versa!!

9. **Cash breakeven is an Essential Milestone.** The reason for emphasising this, is based on my years of experiencing this short sightedness with entrepreneurs and founders. It may not appear significant or important in the scheme of things,

and constant comparisons with some visible players, who are possibly worse off, only lulls you into thinking so! That unfortunately, is far from the truth. If you do not work towards a finite time frame of cash breakeven, you are only running a cost centre which keeps burning more and more cash, and any investor will at some stage wake up to it, and seek or force corrective action. Those actions could have far reaching, damaging consequences, for the venture and you. There are examples of this, if you spend some time to look around and do some secondary knowledge gathering. It is against the basic tenet of the business and the investment, as the returns for the investor can only happen if there is appreciation of Enterprise Value, and that is purely driven by the belief and reassurance that the organization will turn the corner and make money, someday, somehow, sometime! The time horizons may vary, and in some cases extend to decades, but there is always a finite time frame for this. Don't get carried away by the rhetoric that we are in the valuation game. Every valuation has to have a basis, and the basis for valuing an enterprise is its ability to grow, acquire customers and make money. Often, future cash flows are used as the cornerstone of valuation! For each and every venture and business, the cash breakeven often means greater leeway to fund and manage growth and expansion better. Let that be your driver. Set your own standards for this. The journey of each venture is individually different and unique, and drawing comparisons is something that you need to steer clear of!! Let your own vision and goals, drive this for you and the venture! Set a deadline, establish a milestone, and go for it hammer and tongs!! It will pay off in the long run!!

10. **Ensure your Personal Growth keeps Pace.** Probably the last bit of advice, suggestion, or pointer that I can think of, for you as founders. As the business evolves and grows, make the time, effort and commitment to ensure you are also able to grow as a human being, and as a business leader. Leadership of a start-up is a very strange phenomenon; it constantly pushes you out of your comfort zones, and makes you venture into unknown territory; invariably pushing you into sinkholes and pits, that you need to pull yourself out of, only to face the next pitfall. This experience is a steep learning curve, and the best learning will possibly come from the worst experience!! Have often seen promoters and founders fail to keep pace with this demanding journey, and finding

themselves more and more incapable of leading and managing the venture they have created. In all such cases, it often ends in you losing control of your business, either to investors or to competitors. Leaders who cannot make this change happen, to improve themselves, are often sacrificed at the altar of incompetence. Use your mentors, advisors, appoint a coach and guide, to enable you to make the grade, and keep pace. There is no ignominy in accepting that you need help, to grow and develop. None of us is ever ready for what life throws at us; we either learn to deal with it, or we succumb to it. Equip yourself with the support, knowledge and wherewithal to deal with whatever the journey brings forth. Let your love for your venture and the business, drive you to improve yourself, to do justice to the demands of the ever-changing role and expectations of a leader. As the leader of a rapidly growing, constantly changing, demanding business, and its various challenges, you need to be prepared for the demands it will make of you. Maybe a stretch goal, not impossible, but one that you must push yourself to.

What possibly started as just an idea, over a cup of coffee, soon becomes the reason for existence for most start-up founders. Their passion and energy, drives them to take the leap of faith, to establish the venture and convert it, in to a thriving business. This venture soon develops legs of its own, and often ends up driving the founders, pushing them down the road, in this challenging journey of becoming a successful enterprise.

This journey, is fraught with looming threats from unknowns, of treacherous chasms, and unexpected pitfalls. Every entrepreneur who starts one, deserves all the help and support he or she can get, to negotiate this arduous and often chaotic and stressful adventure, if one can call it that. Any tips, pointers, suggestions, that can make it easier, should be the responsibility of all of us, who have more experience and knowledge, to guide and handhold them. It is our prime contribution, as part of this ecosystem, and involved in it, to help them in as many roles, ways and manner as possible!!

I have presented here, what I believe are some of the key challenges & pitfalls, with some tactics and strategies, for preparing yourself as founders of start-ups, to better deal with them. By no means is this list exhaustive, as each journey is unique and often throws up new unanticipated challenges, which may require fresh thinking, and strategies to counter. The adrenaline rush that most individuals who get drawn into this, get, is probably the challenge of the unknown, the sense of adventure and excitement of the journey!! Some tools and techniques to be better prepared to face it, negotiate it and enjoy it more, is what I have tried to put forth.

As entrepreneurs and founders, each one of you is clearly setting out to make your own unique destiny, and this endeavour deserves to be shored up with all the confidence and support that can be garnered. This book hopes to do that, by way of suggestions and pointers, as well as a download of possible challenges and pitfalls, to help make you more prepared and effective. So please go out and do what drives you, and hopefully some of the pointers and thoughts in this book, will enable and make your journey more meaningful and enjoyable!! More importantly, contribute its mite to enhance the probability of the venture's and your success!!

GLOSSARY OF TERMS AND PHRASES

1. **Proof of Concept.** The idea of the product or service remains a hypothesis only, till you actually do a real-time test on a few customers. This helps us convince ourselves and demonstrate that it works. This exercise is referred to as the **Proof of Concept**.

2. **Skin in the Game.** This term refers to the concept that all of us, as human beings, tend to put in more effort and show better commitment, if we have a personal stake in the activity and its outcome. This personal stake is referred to as our **skin in the game**.

3. **Musts and Wants.** In all our desires, we humans have a long list of what we want. Often, some of our Wants may not be critical to our survival or success, but a personal need to acquire. Musts are those desires that are definitely so, to ensure our survival and success.

4. **Credibility Gap.** A new individual, player, Organization or Venture has no references to provide from customers who have used and experienced their product or service. While we may have the best-in-class capabilities and delivery, there is always scepticism and a question mark around the confidence in your offering. This is what is referred to as the **Credibility Gap.**

5. **No Free Lunches.** Every transaction, interaction or decision has its pros and cons, and we do not get everything our way, in our life and businesses. There is a trade-off, set-off, give and take, where we do give up something to get what we like, want or desire. Nothing comes free of all strings. This reality or truth is often referred to as **No free Lunches.**

6. **Fit for Purpose.** In our quest to meet our own, or customer requirements from a product or service, we at times make the mistake of over delivering and hoping we delight the customer. The business economics may not permit, or the customers' wants may not extend to what you provide. This may result in customers not seeing the value, and hence not willing to pay the price for the additional benefits you are delivering. A knife and

sword both cut, but for cutting a cake a knife is all you need. The knife is **Fit for Purpose**.

7. **Bias for Action.** In our effort to get going, we often tend to get caught up in a series of activities, so much so that we think we are not doing anything if we are not constantly in a physical or mental activity. At times, it becomes counter-productive. This constant need to keep ourselves busy with a series of actions, is called a **Bias for Action**.

8. **Living in the Day.** The propensity to keep our time frame horizon limited to today, and not thinking about tomorrow or the future, and the ramifications and impact of our actions today, or worrying about critical events and junctures coming up, is what is referred to as **Living in the Day.**

9. **Spreading too Thin.** In our attempt to get going and moving on, we tend to, at times, take on too many things, and as a result are often unable to do justice to all of them. The outcome is incomplete results, poor execution on some, sub-optimal delivery, and a poor-quality perception as a consequence. This phenomenon of trying to do too much, is what is referred to here.

10. **Here and Now Fallacy**. Another behaviour driven by the need to get going, it often translates into wanting to do everything today and right now. Prioritization, appreciation of urgent versus important, tends to take a back seat. It also results in decisioning which is sub-optimal, as the information needed to take a quality decision, was not available at that moment, and one did not think it appropriate to wait for it.

11. **Efficiency Mindset.** Once businesses start to grow and scale, the efficiencies of scale start to show up in terms of costs savings, profit improvement, and productivity. More is produced, sold more efficiently, as people learn the process and improve on ability to do things faster, cheaper and more consistently. The business then tends to rely on efficiency alone to keep improving on profitability and volumes, instead of looking for new opportunities, markets, products, or customer segments. This is referred to as the **Efficiency Mindset**.

12. **Teeth to Tail ratios**. The ratio of revenue-generating and customer-facing employees to back-end processing and functional support employees is what is referred to as **Teeth to Tail Ratio**. Often the cause of imbalance, it remains

the ratio to watch, in a fast-growing Venture, to ensure the engine for growth, the revenue generating and customer facing group or 'teeth', is adequately planned for and staffed.

13. **Devils Advocate**. A person who deliberately chooses to question all assumptions and parameters and outputs in a plan, to ensure adequate scrutiny and questioning is done to all of it, thus making it intrinsically more robust, is referred to as the **Devil's Advocate**. It is often played by one or more members in a team, to provide rigour and adequate discussion.

14. **Survivors' Bias.** We tend to look at the successful and read about projects, ventures and people, as they are more prominent and visible, and assume that it is easy and doable for most of us. Cricketers, movie stars, start-ups, senior executives, are seen, and we assume if so and so can make it, it must be easy. We cannot see the huge numbers that get buried under the competition, stress, challenges and die a natural death along the way. Our thoughts and beliefs are coloured by what is visible. This is called the **Survivors' Bias**.

15. **Visit to the Cemeteries**. Another phrase to emphasize the need to look at those businesses and ventures that have failed consciously, to understand

what does not work and is to be guarded against. Looking at successes alone, and learning what went right sometimes makes things appear far rosier than the reality. Consciously seeking and looking at failed and dead businesses, provides a better perspective and the complete picture. This is referred to as a **visit to the cemeteries**.

16. **Value Proposition**. Often used as a term to help identify the unique value that the product or service delivers to the customer, which helps differentiate this offering from others in the market place. Any offering needs to have a strong enough value proposition for the customer, which compels them to purchase your product or service. It holds true for negotiations as well, as a good value proposition helps in closing the same in your favour, and getting the other party to accept your offering.

17. **Keeping up with the Joneses.** Competing with neighbours, peer groups, competitors and even friends, to replicate what they have managed to achieve or consciously benchmark against them, is a behaviour trait that often tends to lead us down the path of doom. This is often referred to as trying to **Keep up with the Joneses**. Prudent to remember that each one's journey and experiences

are different and trying to do something because someone else is also doing it, is not a wise approach.

18. **First mover Advantage.** Being the first to identify a new product or service or business opportunity and acting upon it to enter the market, is clearly an advantage in busines terms, as it allows you to build and scale the venture, to establish yourself early in the space. This is referred to as the **first mover advantage**.

19. **Cart before the Horse**. Attempting to create and launch a business project before an idea is even fully conceptualized or tested, is called putting the **cart before the horse**. You do need a product or service that the customer wants and is willing to pay for, before you can launch a venture. The market opportunity and customer need should drive the business, and not vice versa.

20. **Chain as strong as the Weakest Link.** In a series of processes and events, where one follows the other sequentially, to produce an outcome, the quality, speed and consistency of the output will always be driven by the poorest quality, speed or consistency of any input in the chain. To produce a dish in a restaurant, the poor quality and speed of the preparation in terms of cutting vegetables will

be detrimental to good and timely food getting on the table. This is referred to the weakest link. Designing processes to deliver an output, calls for ensuring every link is equally strong to meet the standard of output desired.

21. **Boot Strapping.** This is a term used to describing the process where, in early-stage ventures, the founders pool together their meagre savings and scarce resources, to somehow put together a business which can be up and running. It often means working out of temporary office space, working off floors, scrounging to put together enough to do a proof of concept, short staffed and working stretch hours, to somehow make it happen.

22. **Pay per Hour.** This refers to the practice of using resources, infrastructure, services and privileges, as part time, or on an hourly basis, in times of scarcity and stressed budgets. It enables the venture to get the services it needs, while not committing to a fixed pay-out for a month or year, thus keeping the costs down and within the meagre resources at the venture's disposal.

23. **Black Swan Event.** A totally unanticipated event, with an extremely remote chance of happening; is

not something any business or person plans for. In the unforeseen circumstance of that happening, all plans and strategies really go out of the window, and often leaves us at a loss with no plan B or C to deal with it. The recent pandemic is one such event, which put economies in jeopardy, pushing the governments to the wall, in most cases. The rarity of such events is akin to seeing a Black Swan, hence its often referred to as a **black swan event.**

24. **Line of Credit.** This refers to the practice that banks follow, of approving a limit up to which a business may borrow, subject to the working capital need meeting justification. Thus, the venture may use the amount, maximum as per the defined limit, as a borrowing, provided the borrowing conditions are met. This flexible borrowing limit is often spoken of as **the line of credit.**

25. **Acceptable Ageing.** Another frequently used term by banks and lending institutions, it refers to what the bank or institution will accept as a reasonable and valid period for delayed payment from the customers, for a business which is borrowing for working capital. Invoices which customers do not pay within their defined time period, are thus assumed as bad debts by them, and hence they

do not allow the venture to borrow against such due invoices. The period as defined by them for acceptable and valid dues from customers, which is normally between 90 and 120 days, is called **acceptable ageing.**

26. **Emotional Blinkers.** Being too close to the action, and getting emotionally involved with the business or venture, often results in us starting to see things with the emotional colours and hues. It makes us see things not as they are, but through an emotional pair of coloured lenses, thus distorting our perception of what actually is. We either ignore or overestimate some, or all factors in what we see. This is called viewing the situation with **emotional blinkers.**

27. **Idea Obsession.** As owners of ideas, we tend to at times get too attached to it, often to the detriment of the venture or business. It can result in persisting with it, when the tests or data shows there are lacunae and shortcomings. Escalates costs, creates frustration, leads to confrontation with partners and associates, and creates needless heartburn as we get obsessed with it and do not drop a bad one. This behaviour is referred to as **idea obsession.**

28. **Missing the woods for the Trees.** Being too close to the action, at times we tend to get caught up in the details and fail to see the bigger picture in total perspective. This is what is termed as **missing the woods for the trees.** Always good to distance oneself and see it from a total perspective, before taking a decision which could impact the venture or business.

29. **Intellectual Fatigue.** If we are constantly faced with challenges, which calls for involved thinking, and we deal with the stress of all thoughts being questioned or written off by bosses, or partners, we often tend to give up earlier and not stretch ourselves to do the thinking. We let others drive the decision making and go along, even when we have a different point of view, just to avoid confrontation. This phenomenon is called **intellectual fatigue.**

30. **Control Fixation.** As leaders and founders, we often have the constant need to stay in control, to give ourselves in the chaos, a sense of stability. It results in the need to micro-manage, and instead of letting go, as the venture grows in size, people and competence, we become obsessed more and more with taking all decisions. This behaviour

is termed as **control fixation.** Empowerment, delegation and exception management takes a back seat, when that is really what is called for in the venture.

31. **Sunk Cost Conundrum.** Business decisions don't always go right; there are times when we chase wrong ideas, push wrong products, hire wrong people or run wrong campaigns, at significant costs and wastage of resources. This makes us as leaders and busines owners, at times, resort to trying to make it work, as we believe we have already spent a large sum of money in coming thus far with it. This is termed the **sunk cost conundrum.** It can result in spending good money behind bad, as we continue to back a lost cause.

32. **Cutting your Losses.** Related to the above, this refers to the need to consciously take a decision not to continue to back a bad idea, plan, activity or person, but take the tough call of putting an end to it, or terminating it. By doing so, you are ensuring you do not keep spending valuable resources, time or money behind what is a lost case. You are essentially **cutting your losses**, when you do so.

www.ingramcontent.com/pod-product-compliance
Lightning Source LLC
Chambersburg PA
CBHW020903180526
45163CB00007B/2604